"What an unbelievable story! Not only will you love reading it, but . . . you will also find yourself lifted to a new level in your experience with God and in your desire to serve Him."

C. Peter Wagner, Chancellor
Wagner Leadership Institute

"Albert Runge, a seasoned storyteller, recounts the story of his Jewish family with pathos and humor—much like any Rabbi would. I am thrilled to discover the details of this amazing testimony, as it was the very ministry I now lead that helped Al Runge come to know Jesus as his personal Savior. . . . But this is more than the story of a man of God—it is a story about God Himself. Throughout these pages you will see the presence of God and be . . . blessed."

Dr. Mitch Glaser, President
The Chosen People Ministries

"I laughed, shed some tears and in the end expressed gratitude to God for His marvelous grace in saving and using a Jewish boy like Albert Runge."

Dr. Gordon Cathey, Pastor

"This is an almost unbelievable account of how an unlikely young Jewish boy found God and of the power of that same God in molding and making him into a 'repairer of walls' who has pastored some of the largest churches in our denomination."

Dr. Peter Nanfelt, President
The Christian and Missionary Alliance

"I couldn't stop reading this wonderful, moving testimony . . . filled with struggle, humor, passion and biblical truth. . . . A modern-day classic."

Dr. Tom Stebbins, Executive Vice President
Evangelism Explosion

"Al Runge's story of faith and the power of God motivates us to believe God, not for the ordinary, but for the extraordinary. Definitely a must read."

Dr. Franklin Pyles, President
The Christian and Missionary Alliance, Canada

A BROOKLYN JEW MEETS JESUS

A Brooklyn Jew Meets Jesus

The Life and Ministry of Albert Abram Runge

Albert Abram Runge

Christian Publications
3825 Hartzdale Drive, Camp Hill, PA 17011
www.cpi-horizon.com
www.christianpublications.com

Faithful, biblical publishing since 1883

A Brooklyn Jew Meets Jesus
ISBN: 0-87509-889-4
LOC Control Number: 2001-130441

Printed in the United States of America

04 05 5 4 3 2

Cover Design by Randall Stahl

This book is dedicated to Johanne Lee Runge,
my wife of forty-eight years. She is my soulmate,
best supporter and faithful companion in ministry.
Every congregation we have served together considers
her the perfect pastor's wife, but more important than
that is our children and grandchildren's emulation
of her love and genuine spirituality.
I thank God every day for Lee.

This is what the LORD says:

"Let not the wise man boast of his wisdom
or the strong man boast of his strength
or the rich man boast of his riches,
but let him who boasts boast about this:
that he understands and knows me,
that I am the LORD, who exercises kindness,
justice and righteousness on earth,
for in these I delight," declares the LORD.
(Jeremiah 9:23-24)

Contents

FOREWORD

I have known Albert Runge for fifty-four years. I remember the morning in 1944 when a sixteen-year-old Jewish boy came into the Brooklyn Alliance Tabernacle church where I was the pastor. Albert had accepted Jesus as his Messiah and was looking for a church where he could grow in his faith in Jesus. He didn't have the five-cent fare for the trolley car so he walked a great distance through a tough neighborhood to get to the church for the Sunday services and midweek prayer meeting.

He was a sight to behold: skinny, underfed, poorly dressed, wearing thick eyeglasses highlighting his uncoordinated eyes. His hair went in several different directions and his protruding teeth exaggerated his smile. What he lacked in physical appearance was surpassed by his spiritual fervor. He was truly on fire for the Lord. He engaged himself in giving out gospel literature in his Jewish community. One time when he gave a man a tract, the man took a few steps away and began to read, then turned and without warning spit in Albert's face. Al replied, "God bless you, brother, for this shower of blessing!" Albert considered persecution an opportunity to build treasures in heaven.

He was in reality a gem in the rough. No one in the congregation ever expected Albert to do anything significant in life. He was not someone who would be voted "most likely to succeed" in his high school yearbook. He flunked out of high school!

Albert's one significant talent was a childlike trust in God. By faith, a few years later, he returned to high school and then went on to college and seminary and finally into the ministry. Over the years, Albert Runge has been an accomplished leader under the anointing of God's Spirit.

The fascinating details of his life story and how the Lord Jesus made his life meaningful are before you in this book. If God can use Al Runge to do great things for the kingdom of God, He can use anyone who will trust Him with his life.

Enjoy this true story of God's grace and power in the life of an unlikely candidate for success!

Dr. Eugene Quinn McGee
President of the Home Bible Study Radio Ministry

INTRODUCTION

Brothers, think of what you were when you were called. Not many of you were wise by human standards; not many were influential; not many were of noble birth. But God chose the foolish things of the world to shame the wise; God chose the weak things of the world to shame the strong. He chose the lowly things of this world and the despised things—and the things that are not—to nullify the things that are, so that no one may boast before him. It is because of him that you are in Christ Jesus, who has become for us wisdom from God—that is, our righteousness, holiness and redemption. (1 Corinthians 1:26-30)

A lifetime is a step-by-step journey from birth to death and into eternity. We are born into a world full of confused people who are groping to find some meaning for their lives. Instinctively we seek a rationale for the way things are.

An important question to a Jew is how to remain Jewish in a world dominated by non-Jews. Gentiles find it difficult to understand how much it means for a Jew to be a Jew. Rabbinical tradition has instilled in the Jewish community the belief that Jews can't remain Jewish and at the same time believe that Jesus is the promised Messiah. A Jewish couple that I knew was investigating the messianic claims of Jesus of Nazareth. They decided, however, to forsake their inquiry because they were told that they could not remain Jews if they accepted Jesus. Their decision was not based on theological considerations or whether Jesus is the true Jewish Messiah, but on the fear that they would be separated from the Jewish community.

When a Jew becomes a Christian, some will consider him a renegade, a traitor and an enemy to his own people. Fortunately, that viewpoint is changing. Many Jewish people are becoming believers in Jesus while retaining their Jewish identity. They refuse to be intimidated by the negative opinion of others.

When I came to Christ in 1943, I thought I was the only Jew in the world who believed in Jesus. My uncle was disgusted with me. He asked me, "How could you, a Jew, believe in Jesus when His followers mistreated our family so badly in Russia?"

I answered, "For a very logical reason. Jesus is our Jewish Messiah; therefore, it is my duty as a Jew to believe in Him, even if the entire nation of Israel doesn't agree with me. Remember, the majority of our people were often in the wrong. In the days of Moses, only two Jews, Joshua and Caleb, believed God and were allowed to enter the Promised Land. Our people wanted to stone Moses to death and appoint another leader to take them back to Egypt and slavery. They had forgotten their oppression. The fact that elements of the Christian church are in apostasy and misrepresent Jesus by their evil behavior doesn't discredit Him, even as Israel's unbelief doesn't discredit God's faithfulness."

Many Jews have been repelled from Jesus because of the anti-Semitic hostility of those who falsely claim to follow Him. The first few years of my life, I did not know that Jesus loved me.

It wasn't easy going against the strong currents of the beliefs of my community, but through Jesus I have found true meaning in my life. Journeying with God does not mean there are all successes and no failures, all joys and no sorrows, all pleasures and no sadness; nor does it mean that we never stray. It does mean that He is always there by our side, never leaving or forsaking us. He taught me some important lessons, many of which I learned by making mistakes. There were times that the Lord Jesus had to take me by my hand and lead me back to the right path for my life.

The wondrous truth is that we were created to walk with God. While the Scripture speaks of walking with God, it never speaks of God walking with us. He takes the lead. We must follow Him. Every day I find Him a faithful companion and friend, and every day my faith grows stronger. My greatest discovery has been that God wants only two responses from me: my love and my trust. If we love Jesus, we will seek to please Him, and if we trust Him, we will follow His guidance. He deserves our love and trust because His love is trustworthy.

My story is a testimony of God's goodness and mercy toward me. My life corresponds to what King David wrote: "Surely goodness and mercy shall follow me all the days of my life: and I will dwell in the house of the LORD for ever" (Psalm 23:6, KJV).

Jesus accepted me as I was, without any apparent potential for success. If it weren't for Him, I would have lived a disappointed and wasted life. He nourished me with His lovingkindness. His restoring power made my life worthwhile.

Being a Jew is very important to me, because that is who I am. As I relate my spiritual journey, it is my prayer that you, my reader, will come to understand that Jesus is the Jewish Messiah and the Savior of the world.

CHAPTER ONE

My Jewish Heritage

This day I call heaven and earth as witnesses against you that I have set before you life and death, blessings and curses. Now choose life, so that you and your children may live and that you may love the LORD your God, listen to his voice, and hold fast to him. For the LORD is your life, and he will give you many years in the land he swore to give to your fathers, Abraham, Isaac and Jacob. (Deuteronomy 30:19-20)

When I was a boy in elementary school, one of my uncles felt very sorry for me. He said to my mother, "Anna, Albert has very little possibility of ever amounting to much. He is an asthmatic with many allergies, and he has poor eyesight. He has few academic skills and doesn't appear to have any unusual intellectual or artistic talents. When he is old enough, I can help him rent a newsstand in the subway. It isn't much of a future, but at least he will make a living."

Imagine what my life might have been like! Each day before the sun rose in the sky, I would have gone down into New York City's dingy subway system to open up my newsstand. I would have sold newspapers, cheap magazines, tobacco products and chewing gum. After sunset and the rush hour were over I would have returned, weary, to my apartment. None of my customers could even dream of the useful life that I might have lived if I had discovered the Holy One of Israel, the Promised One. Through Him, I found the blessing of the God of Abraham upon my life. Over my lifetime, I have discovered more and more of God's never-ending love. This is what my story is about.

I have often wondered about my forefathers. What kind of people were they? What did they accomplish in their lives? What were their stories? How did their lives affect mine? My curiosity about them drove me to begin writing my own life story for my four children and eleven grandchildren.

A Rabbinic Legacy

My mother was proud of being the daughter of a rabbi. She delighted in talking about him because she adored him. However, when I asked her questions about her childhood, she tenaciously refused to answer. "I don't want to remember my unhappy childhood. Only the present is important," she would reply with sadness in her eyes. Aunt Rose, my mother's older sister, explained my mother's hesitancy to talk about her childhood. She told me, to the best of my recollection, "Our family emigrated from Russia to escape the government-backed anti-Jewish riots. Our parents finally decided to flee Russia for America. We left all our assets behind.

"Your mother was only six years old when we arrived on Ellis Island with only the clothes we were wearing. The stern, unsmiling immigration officer on Ellis Island looked us over and asked us many difficult questions. We children were afraid that he was going to send us back to Russia and not allow us into America. We did not want to be sent back to our persecutors. We were relieved to pass all the tests and enter the U.S. It was the fulfillment of our dream of the Promised Land.

"Four years later, tragedy hit our family. Both of our parents died in the deadly influenza epidemic of 1918 that killed over 20 million people worldwide. We became orphans. Various relatives took us in and we were separated from one another. Promising to raise your mother as their own daughter, distant relatives took her into their home.

"But they broke their promise. They took her out of the fourth grade and compelled her to work for her room and board as their servant. That is why your mother doesn't want to remember her unhappy childhood."

The older I get, the more I desire to know about my ancestry. While in Tel Aviv, I visited the Museum of the Jewish Diaspora where efforts are being made to identify and restore the genealogies of Jewish families. I asked the computer operator on duty if she knew the origin and meaning of my mother's maiden name, "Barkan."

"Oh yes," she replied immediately, not even checking it on the computer. "It means a son of a priest."

"Well, my mother had told me that I descended from the high priestly family, but I didn't believe her," I responded.

"What! You didn't believe your mother? Your own mother?" she queried me. A number of bystanders jumped in to chide me for doubting my mother.

"I thought my mother was just doing some wishful thinking," I said, trying to defend myself. "She told me only once!"

My maternal grandfather was a trained rabbi, as were his forefathers. Rabbinical leadership was a family tradition for us in Russia for many generations. My mother told me that I was a direct descendant of a miracle-working rabbi. A segment of religious Jews still venerate such a rabbi for his supernatural, miracle-working powers. They believe those who know how to pronounce the forgotten pronunciation of God's personal name can perform miracles. They call such a powerful rabbi *Baal Shem Tov*, which means "master of the good name."

While in Israel, I heard a story of a descendent of the most famous *Baal Shem Tov*. He made his ancestry known on a plane while flying toward Israel. The word quickly spread among the passengers. Many jumped from their seats, rushing toward him for his blessing. The pilot ordered them all back to their seats in order to keep the plane balanced. Whether the story is true or not, I can't say, but it indicates how highly many Jews revere the memory of such a rabbi.

My mother told me never to forget that I was a Jew. She related the last words of her dying father on his sick bed. He took his grieving ten-year-old daughter's hand, placed it over his heart and said, "You must promise me that you will die as a Jew, so I can rest in peace." She never went back on her promise. My mother asked me to make the same promise to her. "Remember," she said, "you were born a Jew, and you must die a Jew."

A Father's Pride

My father also had an unhappy childhood. He suffered the misfortune of his parents' divorce when he was just ten years old. His father, Fred Rosenthal, came to America from Germany before the First World War. My headstrong grandmother, Louise Jacobs, married him against her parents' advice. She was in love; whoever he was before she met him did not matter. Later, she discovered that he had served as an officer of the Imperial German Army. During the First World War, the federal authorities did not allow him to leave the city of Brooklyn. They kept an attentive eye on his activities.

My great-grandparents' worst fears were realized. My grandfather broke up their marriage. He remarried and fathered three more children, Albert, Ruth and Eleanor. While my dad still loved his father, he felt like an outsider in his stepfamily.

My grandmother returned to her parents' home with her young son. Her parents stood by their daughter and grandson. My great-grandfather Jacobs was a wealthy merchant. He and his five brothers had established a chain of men's clothing stores called The Six Little Tailors. He was respected as a leading citizen in the city of Brooklyn. My great-grandfather Jacobs was a generous man. Out of his own pocket he hired a contractor to build his local synagogue. My dad always spoke well of his grandparents.

At sixteen years of age, my father won the title of the second strongest man in New York City at a YMCA citywide contest. I heard many stories about my dad's youthful strength and temper. My Aunt Ruth, his half sister, told me about his exploits of strength. When she was a little girl she bought a piece of watermelon from a street merchant sitting on a horse-drawn wagon loaded with melons. She took a bite and it had a bitter taste. My dad politely asked the man to refund his sister's money or give her a better slice of watermelon. He angrily refused, waving his knife over his head in defiance, yelling profanities and threatening my father.

"I watched your father walk to the back of the wagon," Aunt Ruth told me. "With brute strength, he lifted the rear of the loaded-down wagon up off the ground and turned it over. I stood there flabbergasted. I could not believe my very own eyes." She went on to depict the scene, "The man, his horse and his wagon fell down, and his watermelons splattered all over the street. In the commotion we ran away before the police arrived."

Later my dad joined the army, and after his discharge, he hopped a freight train to see America. In one town he accepted a challenge to fight the local champion boxer. He agreed with some gamblers to take a dive. However, his temper flared up when the other fighter didn't pull his punches. My dad knocked him out cold. He got out of town fast.

After marrying my mother, my father went to Detroit to look for a job. Outside the Ford plant, he waited patiently in a long line of unemployed men for his turn to get a job. The personnel manager asked for his name. "My name is Charles Rosenthal," he replied with an eager grin on his face.

"Sorry, all the jobs are taken!" he was told. Disappointed, my dad stepped out of the line. As he was walking away, he glanced back and noticed the other men in the line behind him were getting hired. Later that night, he figured out that Jews weren't wanted. The next day, he went back to try again. This time he gave the name of his Gentile friend. He told the foreman his name was Charles Runge and got a job. I read the letter he had sent to his mother explaining his name change. My dad assured her he wasn't ashamed of being Jewish. He had changed his name just to get work.

A Difficult Beginning

I came into the world on November 21, 1928, at 2 o'clock in the morning. My birth weight was 13 pounds 6 ounces. My mother often told me with her Yiddish accent, "You vere a blue baby, ve almost lost you at birth." Then tears filled her eyes as she told me of her labor of love: "I vent down into the valley of the shadow of death to give you life. Oy! Did I hurt? Always remember your mother is your best friend." She was my best friend to her dying day.

On the eighth day of my life, I entered into the covenant of Israel through circumcision. My parents gave me the Hebrew name Abram. If my dad had kept our family name, I would be known today as Albert Abram Rosenthal. My mother assured me that a great feast had celebrated my entrance into the covenant of Abraham. "We had all our relatives and neighbors there to celebrate your circumcision. We had rye, pumpernickel and fresh rolls, along with blintzes, corn beef, salami, brisket of beef, kosher pickles, sour tomatoes, cheesecake and whipped cream cakes of all kinds. Oy! You cost us a fortune."

My father became a sick man and was unable to work. My mother explained that during the First World War, while my father was fighting in France, his unit had been bombed with mustard gas, which caused his physical disability. My dad admitted that his big mistake was his impatience to get discharged from the army. He skipped out of his final physical examination. In the years that followed, he persistently tried to persuade the government that his illness was due to his war experience, but to no avail. The Veteran Administration denied him a full disability pension.

I am sure his disability added to the frustration of not being able to work. In Jewish culture, manliness is measured by how well a man supports his family. He wanted to provide adequately for us and it hurt him not to be able to do it. I still remember a little red wagon that I loved pulling around the block, playing delivery truck with it. When we moved to another apartment my father gave away my wagon to the moving man's helper because he did not have any money to tip him.

"That's my wagon!" I protested as loudly as I could. My dad promised me a better one. As time passed by, I became impatient. Finally, he took me to a toy store to pick out a new wagon, but to my disappointment, my dad said it was too expensive and that I was getting too old for a wagon. I had to do without one. I stopped complaining when I saw the shame in his eyes.

In spite of my father's inability to provide for our family, my mother never tolerated any disrespect toward him. When times were tough, we children blamed our dad for the family's misfortune. My mother admonished us always to respect our father and remember that he gave us life. I realize now that the divorce of my dad's parents and his illness defeated his spirit and blighted his life.

I grew up in the Great Depression. From my earliest recollections we were on state welfare. In those days it was called "charity." The welfare investigators made surprise inspections, especially at dinnertime. They liked peeking into the cooking pots on the stove to see what we were having for dinner. They wanted to be sure we were truly in need. It should have been obvious—we lived in a cockroach-infested flat without central heat or hot water. I slept in the living room on an old couch inhabited by bedbugs. Every night I woke up itching from bites. No matter how many I caught and killed each night, there were always more to kill the next day. My parents sympathized with my predicament, but they didn't have any money for a new couch.

Living on the charity of the state made us feel like beggars. To improve our circumstances, my mother took advantage of a new federal program to train welfare recipients for work. She became a practical nurse, taking us off welfare. My mother became the proud breadwinner of the family. Her first paycheck restored our self-respect. Only one other time did I see her face light up with such pride; it was the day she became an American citizen.

A Mother's Love

The streets of Brooklyn back then were safe for children. The Jewish mothers of our block kept an eye on all the children and periodically checked up on their whereabouts. Woe to any stranger who appeared on our block and got too friendly with the children. When it comes to protecting their children, the wrath of Jewish mothers is awesome.

I had the freedom to roam on our block as long as I didn't cross the street or go around the corner. Crossing the street without my mother was a major transgression. Most of the day I was on my own to play with my friends whom I suspected were also stool pigeons. We couldn't get away with any misbehavior. The news would spread from child to mother and from mother to mother. We children knew there were always eyes on us. My mother put the fear of God in me: "You may fool your mother, but you can't trick God. He sees everything you are doing, so you better be good." At mealtimes and before dark, the Jewish mothers would stick their heads out of the windows and yell for their children to come in. There was no quiet until all the children were safe at home. If a child didn't show up on time, the whole neighborhood went on a search and rescue mission.

My mother was a model of virtue. She never lied to me. If I asked questions she didn't want to answer or felt weren't any of my business, she replied with an old Yiddish saying, "Ask me no questions and I will tell you no lies." She also warned me, "The punishment of a liar is that no one will ever believe him."

My mother demonstrated true faithfulness and sacrificial love for her husband and children. I remember my mother giving me her portion of meat, denying herself and pretending she wasn't hungry because I had insensitively asked for more. She would proudly proclaim, "My children are my treasure and joy." My mother's example taught me unselfishness and respect for others. She often said, "There is no disgrace in being poor, but there is a disgrace in being a thief."

One day, my mother overheard me using a curse word. I never saw my mother move so fast. She grabbed me before I could get away and dragged me, struggling and screaming, into the bathroom. There she washed my mouth out with a bar of hard yellow laundry soap and did not stop until I threw up my lunch. She demanded that I apologize to her and God for using profanity. She made me promise never to use a dirty word again. That experience cleaned up my language for good. I thank God for her dignity, integrity and faithful love.

My mother desired to live as an orthodox Jew, overseeing a kosher kitchen, but she wasn't always successful. I remember her storm of protest over my father bringing home a ham sandwich. To the best of her ability she lived out her beliefs. On one occasion, my mother was cleaning the house of a wealthy woman. She was fed a hot dog at lunch and then her employer laughingly told my mother it was pork. My mother gagged and threw up on the woman's expensive Turkish carpet. Even though my mother lost her job, she was proud that her kosher stomach had rejected the pork.

My Inferiority Complex

I had my reasons for feeling inferior compared to other children. I had asthma, an illness that kept me indoors a lot. Before the invention of television, the streets belonged to the kids. Each season had its games. In the fall and winter we boys played marbles and Johnny-on-the-pony while the girls played jacks and hopscotch. In the spring the boys made scooters with empty wooden orange crates, nailing them to a two-by-four and attaching roller skates as wheels. The girls skated in the streets. In the summer the boys played stickball while the girls skipped rope.

Many times I sat by the window looking down at the other children playing in the street, wishing I could be with them. I remember one of my good days when I was allowed to play in the street. I was hoping to get selected on a team to play stickball. One kid after the other was chosen before me until I was one of the last two yet to be chosen. The two self-appointed captains got into an argument. "You take him."

"No, you take him."

The loser got me for his team. In one game, I hit a lucky home run right out of sight. The next game the captains were fighting over me as their first choice. That sure helped my ego.

My mother tried to help me understand why I could not play every day by saying, "You aren't like other children. You are a sick boy." I can recall sitting for hours at the clinic of Kings County Hospital every Tuesday morning for allergy tests and injections. The physician said I was allergic to cats, dogs and animals of all kinds, dust, cigarette smoke, tomatoes, milk, cheese and more things than I can remember.

In fact, I seemed to be allergic to myself. My specialist informed my mother, "Mrs. Runge, because your son's breathing is a continuous struggle, I fear that he will likely develop a serious heart condition and not live a long life." Many a night I thought I heard a loud train whistle only to wake up and discover it was my wheezing.

Often in the middle of the night I was rushed by ambulance to a hospital because of a serious asthma attack. I remember on one occasion being in the hospital a few days before Christmas. Feeling very sorry for me, the nurses in my ward promised me a wonderful celebration. They were preparing the biggest party of my life. I anticipated loads of gifts, candy and lots of attention on Christmas Day, but my doctor had another plan for me.

"Don't worry, son," he said. "I am going to do all I can to get you home for Christmas." Attempting to get rid of the mucus from my bronchial tubes and lungs, he pumped pure oxygen into my mouth, trying to open up my breathing passageways, and then he forced disgustingly bitter medicine down my throat, making me throw up. I kept hoping and praying that the compassionate doctor would fail in his efforts to make me well. Finally, after much effort on his part and suffering on mine, my wheezing ceased. With a smile of triumph and a pat on my back, he dismissed me from the hospital into the grateful arms of my mother just two days before Christmas. My dreams of a wonderful, special party just for me went up in smoke. I was one disappointed kid.

Poor eyesight was another disability I endured. For some time, I wasn't even aware of my poor vision. I just assumed the world looked that way naturally. One night, while walking with my family, I fell over something. My father yelled, "Didn't you see the dog?"

I replied, "What dog? I didn't see any dog. Did anyone see a dog?"

My sisters teasingly shouted back, "Of course, stupid, the dog you just fell over! Keep your eyes open!" My father decided to take me to an eye doctor, who discovered my myopic vision and night blindness.

The public school administration then decided to place me in the sight-conservation class. We read from large-print books and wrote with thick lead pencils on unlined paper to avoid eyestrain. I thought my dream had come true, because I had the perfect excuse not to study. All I had to do was complain that my eyes were tired, and my teacher quickly accommodated me by saying, "It is more important to conserve your eyes for your future than to study now." We were also excused from homework. (Years later, the theory behind the class was proven incorrect—eyesight isn't a limited energy resource that can be conserved for later use; the eye is a muscle requiring reasonable exercise to perform properly.)

Learning to Be "Tough"

My father criticized me for not being tough enough for this hard world. He often bragged about his fights as a boy. My dad told me about a fight he had with a schoolmate, giving him two black eyes. The boy's father, a big and rough teamster, went to my dad's grandfather to get some satisfaction. According to my dad's story, his grandfather tried to apologize for Father's behavior, but he wasn't able to reason with the angry man. The outraged father yelled expletives and then made the mistake of calling him a dirty Jew. My great-grandmother, fearing a fight, locked the gate in front of their brownstone house to separate them. My dad proudly said, "My grandfather grabbed hold of the iron gate with his bare hands and literally yanked it out of the cement to get at the man. The big tough teamster turned pale and ran away as fast as he could, dragging his tearful son behind him." My dad criticized me for being too soft. He often chided me, "Why don't you get into a fight and act like a real man?"

Seeking my dad's approval, I started looking for a fight. At school, a big bully kept threatening me in front of the other kids. He was trying to make himself look like a bigshot while making me appear like a helpless coward. "I'm going to beat you up, four eyes," he repeated many times, waving his clenched fist at me. My dad had no sympathy for my plight. "Don't be a victim! Be a man and knock his block off." The school bully kept intimidating me until I finally had enough.

"Meet me in the boy's washroom and we will fight it out," I yelled in the lunch line so all the kids could hear my brave challenge. I wasn't thinking very clearly at the time. The bully was a lot bigger than I was, and he had a reputation of being a tough kid.

The boys' room was packed with excited spectators. There was an overflow crowd of kids waiting for the big fight. We put up our fists. I hit him first in the stomach as hard as I could. To my surprise, my tough opponent dropped his arms to his side and cried like a helpless baby. I hit him a couple more times. The fight ended quickly before a cheering mob. No one in the school ever dared call me "four eyes" again. I got respect in that school, and for the first time my dad bragged about me to his friends. But in my heart, I never felt right about humiliating that boy.

My mother furiously scolded my dad, "What kind of father are you? Are you trying to turn our son into a hoodlum?" My father wasn't able to intimidate my mother with his bad temper over the raising of her children. He knew better than to try to browbeat her when she was defending us.

My Religious Upbringing

Formal religion did not play a very significant role in our family life during my early years. While my father wasn't very religious, he still maintained high moral ideals. Even though he had an unpredictable temper, I never saw my dad intoxicated or involved in an illegal act. He demanded honesty from his children. A lie was a mortal sin to him. When we told him the truth about a misdeed, he rewarded us by not punishing us. My father used to tell me, "Albee, when you look into a mirror, you should see someone you respect."

My parents regarded me as a good and obedient son. I had a very sensitive conscience. One day my mother took my little sister Louise and me to the open-air market. She told us to choose a candy bar to share. Being the son, I thought she wanted me to choose it, and Louise thought it was her choice. My mother paid the merchant for only one candy bar. Unknowingly we each took a candy bar home. When I realized my mistake, I felt like a thief, condemned by God for my sin. My sister laughed it off as an honest mistake to enjoy. I insisted we go back and pay for the extra candy.

As far back as I can remember, even in my earliest childhood, I had a tender heart toward God. I desired to know Him. One motivating drive in my life was to be a good person. I remember telling my mother, who was disappointed with my report cards, "I would rather fail honestly than cheat for good grades." My attitude pleased my mother. God was working in my life, leading me to know Him.

The Unknown Jesus

The only time Jesus was mentioned in our home was when my father went into a temper tantrum. Out of frustration he would bellow, "Jesus Christ!" My mother yelled back equally loud, "Charlie, don't curse in front of the children!"

For a time, I thought His name was profanity. I was seven years old when I heard that Jesus was a real Person. One of my playmates asked me if I was Jewish. "Yes," I replied.

"Well, I am not going to play with you anymore," he said.

"Why not?" I asked.

"Because you crucified Jesus."

I wondered to myself, *Who is this Jesus? What does "crucified" mean?* I thought he must be some kid that I had unintentionally offended.

So I replied, "You are making a mistake, I don't know any kid by the name of Jesus. Introduce him to me and we will work it out."

My playmate looked at me with disbelief and walked away without a word, leaving me in a state of bewilderment.

I asked my mother, "Who is this Jesus that I have been accused of crucifying?" My mother became dead serious. She told me, "Jesus is the God of the Gentiles who taught his people to hate us Jews." She explained, "When I was a little girl in Russia, the Christians broke into our sector of town at Easter time, shouting, "You killed our God, so we can kill you too."

That was my first introduction to Jesus. Much later, I discovered how shamefully the church in Russia misrepresented Jesus. Their wicked actions proved they were not true disciples of Jesus. Our Lord Jesus was a Man of love, peace and nonviolence toward His enemies. Jesus taught His disciples to follow His good example.

He told them, "But I tell you who hear me: Love your enemies, do good to those who hate you, bless those who curse you, pray for those who mistreat you" (Luke 6:27-28).

A Family Tragedy

I am one of four children. My sisters are Louise and Florence. My older sister, Florence, told me the sad story of the death of our brother, Louis.

"One day Dad announced that he was going to visit Grandfather Rosenthal. Louis, our little brother, pleaded to go with him, as little boys do. 'Please, Daddy, please take me with you.'

" 'No!' Dad said firmly, 'I am going to be gone for just a little while. I will be back within the hour.' Louis was very disturbed at being left behind. Mom thought that an ice cream treat would calm him down. Mom told me to take him to the candy store and buy him a cone. I was only seven years old and Louis was four. Louis tried to balance the cone and his ball and hold on to me. He accidentally dropped the ball. It bounced into the street. Before I could stop him, he broke loose from my grip and ran after his ball. Louis never saw the truck that hit him. He died instantly."

On returning home, my father saw the bloody, broken body of his little son lying in the street. Out of shock, he lost his voice for three days. Over the years, Florence has suffered enormous guilt and anguish over that accident.

In my memory, I can dimly recall the unhappy day of my brother's funeral. I can still visualize his little white casket on the dining room table. I can still hear the sobbing of the family and in my mind's eye feel an evil, foreboding presence in that darkened room.

The accident changed our lives and disrupted our family permanently. My parents kept reproaching each other. My mother wondered if God was punishing her. Seeking comfort, my mother asked our rabbi, "Where is Louis now? Is he alive in heaven?" The young, sympathetic rabbi tried to comfort her by saying, "Your son will always live on in your memory." No hope for immortality was given us. Every year on his birthday, my mother lit a memory candle for Louis. She sat silently thinking about her precious little boy until the flame of the candle burned itself out.

The rabbi unintentionally provoked my father by asking for his fee before officiating at the funeral. I am sure that he meant no offense. Over the anguish of the tragedy, my father expressed hostility to God and denounced all religions as moneymaking swindles. He warned me, "All they want is your money." I wondered, *What money?* We didn't have any.

In my parents' grief over the loss of Louis they seemed to forget all about me. They spoke often of Louis in my presence. "How beautiful! How smart! What a good child he was!" I can't ever remember them speaking of me in such glowing terms. My Aunt Hattie meant well by telling me, "God took Louis because he was too good for this world." I wondered why I wasn't good enough to be selected. Why would God take the superior son away leaving the inferior one behind? Over and over again I was reminded that it was Louis who had won a neighborhood baby beauty contest and not me. I felt like an ugly duckling. In time, I accepted my inferiority philosophically and without self-reproach. After all, I couldn't help how I was born.

Beginning of a Spiritual Journey

The tragedy of my brother's death not only upset our family's system, but it also damaged my mother physically. My normally healthy mother came down with rheumatic fever, which could have damaged her heart. During her illness she wasn't able to care for us, so along with my two sisters, we were placed in a Jewish institution for six months. I can barely remember how emotionally upset I was to be in such a strange, unfriendly place so far away from my parents. Florence, my older sister, told me how she was forced by the attendants to clean up after me.

As my mother's health improved, she was able to do some of her own shopping. Every day, on the way to the market, she passed by a building posted with English and Yiddish signs offering free medical treatment in their clinic. Assuming it was a synagogue, my mother took advantage of the free offer. A few days later, a woman visited my mother. She walked up six long flights of stairs to reach our apartment on the top floor. She knocked at our door. "Who is it?" my mother asked from behind a locked door.

Miss Sussdorf replied in Yiddish, "I'm from the clinic across the street." Feeling safe with the stranger, my mother opened the door and invited her in for a cup of hot tea. My mother accepted an invitation from Miss Sussdorf to attend a Christian class. Every Wednesday morning during school hours, a small group of Jewish ladies gathered to socialize, to learn sewing and to study the Bible together.

After Florence, Louise and I returned home, my mother allowed us to attend the children's clubs with one stipulation, "Enjoy all the fun things they provide, but don't believe a word they tell you!" She sternly warned us to be careful not to get converted. We experienced a lot of fun. We especially enjoyed taking their annual boat ride up the Hudson River to Bear Mountain for a picnic. We were taken to the amusement parks at Coney Island. Every Friday night we attended the supper meeting with our mother where we ate kosher hot dogs and sauerkraut for free.

The leader of the boys' camera club was Daniel Fuchs, a Hebrew Christian student from the Biblical Seminary. He not only demonstrated how to take photos and how to develop them in a darkroom, but he also taught us the Bible.

Some Bible stories were familiar to me. I had heard about Abraham, Moses, Joseph and Job before at a synagogue, but I had never heard until then about Jesus being Israel's King Messiah, Son of God and Savior of the world.

Discovering Prayer

Miss Sussdorf radiated undeniable love. Noticing my patched-up school clothes, she purchased an expensive suit for me, the only one I had ever had. It mysteriously disappeared soon after I got it. Later, I asked my mother, "Whatever became of that suit?" She replied, "Your father sold it to a neighbor to put food on the table."

True friendship is one of the most precious gifts that one can receive from another person. Miss Sussdorf was such a friend to our family. She did not forget us, even when we moved to a new neighborhood. Miss Sussdorf faithfully visited my mother once a month. One day on her way to see my mother, she saw me in a playful fistfight. It looked to her like a real street fight. I saw shock on her face and I sensed her distress for me. Something mystifying happened deep within me at that very moment. I felt shame for fighting in front of that good woman. Years later, she told me what she was thinking at the time.

"Albert, when I saw you in a street fight with that ruffian, I lifted up my heart to God and cried out, *Oh Lord Jesus, save Albert from this kind of wild life.*"

God heard and answered her prayer instantaneously. I owe much to Miss Sussdorf, who was a true mother in Israel for me.

The concept of talking to a personal God, who is listening and will answer our prayers, wasn't a part of my early religious training. If my mother spoke of some small happiness in her life, she would quickly knock on wood. I asked her, "Why do you knock on the table?"

"Well," she explained, "you don't want God to hear about your good luck. He may conclude that you are too happy for your own good and send you trouble to keep you humble. I knock on wood to distract God from what I just said."

The Bible tells us in Proverbs 10:22, "The blessing of the LORD makes one rich, and He adds no sorrow with it" (NKJV). I noticed that the people at the mission prayed as though God was a real, living Person who paid attention to them.

When I was about ten years old, Miss Sussdorf asked me, "Albert, have you ever prayed in the name of Jesus?"

"No," I replied. "Why do you ask?"

"Well, if you pray in the name of Jesus, God will answer your prayers." She then quoted a verse from the Bible: "Until now you have not asked for anything in my name. Ask and you will receive, and your joy will be complete" (John 16:24).

I stored her advice away in the back of my mind. A couple of years later, I had an occasion to put her advice to the test. It was Christmas morning of 1940 when my father woke up with severe chest pains and shortness of breath. Unable to get him out of bed, my mother called Dr. Freeman, our family physician, who made house calls. He rushed over to our apartment to examine my father. I overheard him tell my mother, "Mrs. Runge, I regret to tell you this, but your husband has had a massive heart attack. There is nothing I can do for him; he will most likely die before tonight. Make him as comfortable as you can."

We children were sent outside to give him some quiet. On my way to a friend to see what he had received for Christmas, I stopped to pray silently. "Oh God! How could this be happening to my father on the birthday of Your Son, Jesus? If You heal my dad, I will give You my life." Then I ended my prayer in the name of Jesus.

Returning home for lunch, I found my dad sitting at the table eating heartily and looking quite well. He lived for many years to follow. By God's grace, I have kept my commitment to Him.

God's answer to my prayer settled it for me once and for all that Jesus is the true Son of God. From then on, I prayed in the name of Jesus secretly under my covers every night. It was always the same prayer, "Lord, please heal me of my asthma and poor eyesight." Several years passed by before those prayers were answered. In Luke 18:1, "Jesus told his disciples . . . that they should always pray and not give up."

Strange things may happen to those who are seeking God through Jesus. Soon after I began attending the mission, I had a weird nighttime experience. I was fully awake, or so it seemed. Three mysterious shadows appeared, standing by my bedside. One spoke up: "God is too far away to help you. Let us help you." I looked up to heaven and saw a vision of an awe inspiring, stony-faced God sitting on a throne looking away from me. Miss Sussdorf had warned me about deceiving demons. I quickly reacted by stretching up my hands toward heaven and declaring, "I want God!" I said yes to God in Jesus' name and no to those uninvited and unwelcome alien spirits standing by my bedside. I instinctively distrusted those strange intruders in my bedroom. They quickly backed up and disappeared, and I went back to sleep.

I had discovered even before I accepted Jesus as my personal Savior that God is an accessible and present Helper in times of trouble. God is not beyond our reach; He is closer to us than the air we breathe. I came to understand that Satan is the father of lies. If the enemy of our souls isn't able to convince us that God doesn't exist, he will slander God's character. He will try to portray God as a stern, perfectionistic and judgmental person who only cares about judging us who are imperfect. The devil doesn't want us to know that God is love. I am very grateful that Miss Sussdorf taught me to pray in the name of Jesus.

My childhood and early adolescent years were very troublesome for me. I was not prepared to succeed in life. Apart from a miracle, my life was destined for failure. Little did I realize at the time that God was leading me all the way into a future full of His blessings.

CHAPTER TWO

Beginning a New Life

Like newborn babies, crave pure spiritual milk, so that by it you may grow up in your salvation, now that you have tasted that the Lord is good. (1 Peter 2:2-3)

Wartime brought a big change in the ethics and morals of Americans. As a teenager, I was a Western Union messenger boy in the Wall Street area. I often ate at the Buffet Exchange, which operated on the honor system: a customer took whatever he wanted from the food buffet, and as he left the restaurant, he told the cashier what he had eaten and paid for it. No questions were ever asked. A person's word was good enough. The company bragged that the honor system worked well for years. They never lost anything—until after the war. Then the restaurant went bankrupt.

My family moved a lot from one neighborhood to another trying to escape the ever-increasing street crime. When I was fourteen years of age, we moved to Pulaski Street in the Williamsburgh section of Brooklyn. Directly across the street from our new apartment building stood the Gospel Meeting House. Every hot summer evening its doors and windows were opened wide, and all the neighbors could hear their gospel band playing Salvation Army marching music. While passing by on a Sunday evening, I noticed a friendly looking man standing by the front gate welcoming people in with a hearty handshake. Approaching him rather nervously I asked him if could I attend the meeting. "Why, certainly!" he responded enthusiastically, taking my arm and ushering me to a seat. I felt the warm and loving atmosphere of the congregation as soon as I sat down.

The guest preacher was explaining the good news of Jesus and then gave an invitation to receive Christ as a personal Savior. Something strange started happening to me during the invitation. An inner struggle between two opposing forces erupted in a competition for my soul.

One argued against deciding for Jesus; the other was encouraging me to receive Jesus. The adversary logically argued, "Why accept Jesus when you know you are a sinner? Even if all your past sins are forgiven, within a few months you will sin again and be lost forever without any hope. You will be worse off than you are now." He was preying on my self-doubts and insecurity. Just at that moment the preacher declared from the pulpit, "Jesus will forgive you of all your past sins, your present sins and your future sins." He could not have known my inner struggle unless God was speaking to me through him. Those words were good enough for me to decide for Jesus.

Pastor Harry Barger asked those who wanted to accept Jesus as Savior to raise their hands and come forward to the altar. I was too timid to walk down to the altar in a strange place; instead, I rushed home, locked myself in the bathroom for privacy, got down on my knees and prayed. I confessed that I was a sinner, lost without God, and on my way to hell. I realized my spiritual bankruptcy and inability to save myself, so I threw myself upon the mercy and grace of God. I acknowledged that Jesus Christ is the eternal and sinless Son of God. I accepted the fact that Jesus was born of a virgin, and then later was crucified and buried for all my sins. And then He rose from the dead! I acknowledged that Jesus ascended into heaven at the right hand of His heavenly Father and is now interceding on my behalf. I received salvation as a free gift from God. Peace immediately flooded my soul. My struggle was over and I was assured that all my sins were forgiven.

God's Spirit had opened my understanding to the truth of the gospel. There is no other way to explain my theologically insightful conversion. I had a divine encounter with the Spirit of truth, whom Jesus sent to convict the world of sin, of righteousness and of the judgment to come.

The Bible explains what happened to me that night. "For you did not receive a spirit that makes you a slave again to fear, but you received the Spirit of sonship. And by him we cry, 'Abba, Father.' The Spirit himself testifies with our spirit that we are God's children" (Romans 8:15-16).

The joy that came into my heart the night I accepted Jesus was intense and unexplainable. Expecting my family to celebrate my newfound faith with me, I entered the living room to tell them about it as my father, mother and two sisters were listening intently to the radio. I broke their concentration on a soap opera by exclaiming excitedly, "Praise the Lord! I'm saved!" They looked at me like I had lost my mind. My mother broke the tension: "He's just making fun of the Christians."

"No!" I insisted. "I really mean it! I believe in Jesus and I am saved!" My earnestness sent my mother rushing out of the house to the candy store to telephone a relative, who was a psychiatrist. Of course she knew the value of money, and before receiving a service, she always wanted to negotiate the price. Unable to get a good enough family discount, she changed her mind. Returning home, she affectionately patted me on the head, assuring me, "Don't worry, Albee, you will outgrow this." I wasn't worried, and I never outgrew my faith in Jesus. Her hopeful prediction did not come true.

As time went on, my mother said some very harsh things that I know she did not mean in her heart. "I would rather see you a drunk in the gutter than a Christian," she sobbed. Yelling insults did not move me an inch, but her bitter tears and broken heart were harder to overcome. Often she hit me with the big threat: "You are no more a Jew!"

I tried to reason with her. "Mama, if I became an atheist, rejected the existence of the God of Abraham and denied Moses ever existed, would I still be a Jew?"

"Yes, of course!" she quickly replied.

"Well, I still believe in our God, in the Jewish Bible and in the Jewish Messiah. So why can't I still be a Jew and believe in Jesus?"

My mother looked puzzled. "I don't know why," she admitted, "but that is what I was taught as a little girl. You can't believe in Jesus and be a Jew at the same time."

I did not become a Christian because I disliked being a Jew. I agree with the apostle Paul's evaluation of the Jewish nation when he said in Romans 10:2, "For I can testify about them that they are zealous for God, but their zeal is not based on knowledge."

In my Jewish upbringing, I was taught about goodness, honesty and tolerance toward others. My mother used to say, "Where there is no *mensch* (a genuinely good person), be a *mensch*." My mother drilled moral responsibility and ethics into me. I became a Christian not to reject my Jewishness but because I found the God of my fathers through His Son Jesus.

My baptism, without my mother's consent, infuriated her. She threatened to sue the church for brainwashing me.

She told me, "If your rabbi grandfather was alive, he would have a funeral for you. You would be dead to the family. If you weren't just a fourteen-year-old boy, I would throw you out of the house!" Her threats did not frighten me, because I believed if she did, God would take care of me. During this difficult period, God gave me a promise found in the Psalms. "When my father and my mother forsake me, then the LORD will take care of me" (27:10, NKJV).

I replied to my mother's threats by calmly saying, "That's OK, Mama. I will always love you. Even if you throw me out, God, my heavenly Father, will take care of me."

"Oy! I got a *meshugger* (a real nut) for a son, a crazy boy," she replied.

Learning to Walk

Receiving the Lord Jesus completely changed my life, from the inside out. Not only did I believe in Jesus, but I also repented. I acted and thought differently. I discovered that true Christianity is much more than an academic belief system; it is a genuine relationship with the living God through Jesus our Lord. Walking with God fosters intimate fellowship with Him. Noticing the radical change in me, my mother mockingly called me her "little Jesus boy." She could not have paid me a higher compliment.

Becoming a Christian did not transform me into a perfect person as I had hoped. I was born into God's family as a spiritual infant. At first I needed to be fed the milk of God's Word. As a babe in Christ, I wasn't yet ready for the meat of God's Word. In time, I learned how to feed myself and eventually how to feed others with the truth of God. God was patient with me.

No sensible person loses patience with a child because it takes time and practice to walk and talk. Toddlers learn to walk by falling down many times and trying again. A good parent picks up his hurting child, wipes away his tears and comforts him. A mother doesn't say, "Oh, my poor baby, you will never learn, I had better keep you safe in your playpen the rest of your life." No, the mother places her little darling on his feet again and encourages him by saying, "Come to Mama, sweetheart, that's a good boy." She keeps doing it over and over again until her child learns to walk by himself. God is just like a good parent who allows His children to slip, fall and try again in order for them to learn to walk in godly ways. The Bible tells us, "though a righteous man falls seven times, he rises again" (Proverbs 24:16). That has been my experience with God through the years.

Entering a new community of Gentiles was not an easy transition for me. I remember telling God, "Lord, we have a wonderful relationship together. Why do we need to bother with those other Christians?" I was ignorant of the truth of the body of Christ found in First Corinthians 12:13-14: "For we were all baptized by one Spirit into one body—whether Jews or Greeks, slave or free—and we were all given the one Spirit to drink. Now the body is not made up of one part but of many."

I soon discovered that there are no perfect Christians or churches. There were those who unintentionally tried to discourage me. For example, an elder of my church chided me for my youthful zeal. "Albert, you are going so fast in the Christian life, you will meet yourself coming back. It's not normal for a teenager to act like a fanatic. Slow down! Be like my son! Take your time to mature before you try witnessing to others."

Sadly, his son later repudiated the father's Christianity.

The Bible warns us about false teachers and prophets, but sometimes even a well-meaning Christian can mislead us. I became very worried when an elder warned me that I could lose my salvation. He said that if I sinned with a bad thought and failed to confess it before I died, I would be sent straight to hell.

I saw no hope for myself until God gave me an encouraging insight. My mind visualized Jesus on the cross, and I heard Him say, "Since I have suffered so much for you, once I have you, I will never let you go." A sense of security comforted my heart.

I came to understand that the gospel of Jesus Christ is good news for sinners. It would not be good news if one day I was saved and the next day I was lost, if one day God justified me but the next day He condemned me.

As a new Christian, I had enough self-knowledge to fear failing my Lord, so I talked it over with my heavenly Father. "Father, we both know I am an imperfect sinner, I will fail You many times in the future. When I do, please forgive me. Lord Jesus, I am sure I will fail You more than once. Your mercy for me will have to last an entire lifetime."

My prayer was God-given; it assured me of His mercy that is renewed every day. Jesus assured me that if I failed, He would still hold on to me.

When I looked at my life and reflected on all my imperfections, I got quite depressed. In my self-evaluation I didn't amount to much, but seeing myself through God's eyes of infinite love raised my worth beyond my comprehension.

The apostle Paul wrote of the love of Christ in Romans 8:38-39, "For I am convinced that neither death nor life, neither angels nor demons, neither the present nor the future, nor any powers, neither height nor depth, nor anything else in all creation, will be able to separate us from the love of God that is in Christ Jesus our Lord." Because God's love for us is infinite, we have unending value to Him.

Some called me "a diamond in the rough," and surely I had a lot to learn about proper and acceptable behavior. Just after I had become a Christian, I walked along the streets of Brooklyn, singing out hymns like "Blessed Assurance" and "What a Friend We Have in Jesus." People gave me strange looks, but I didn't care, because the music came from my heart. At one evening service, I was singing with gusto along with the congregation when my pastor came down from the platform, walked right over to me and whispered in my ear, "Do you have to sing so loudly?" I was so embarrassed I lost my joy in singing.

I soon became acquainted with petty conflicts in the church. It was disheartening for me to watch Christians disagreeing and hurting each other. The Gospel Meeting House had an active youth group of over sixty young people. We called ourselves the Gospel Bombers. We folded gospel tracts around a piece of candy and wrapped it all in brightly colored cellophane paper. As we drove by in a car, we threw them out of the window at people walking on the street. We called that strategy "bombing people with the gospel." It was great fun. Every Sunday night we met separately from the older people to sing our youthful choruses and songs. Some of the older people were offended and insisted we meet together in one service. The elders said these choruses would amount to nothing and that the youth should sing the great hymns of the church. That was in 1943. The church leadership disbanded our youth group. All of my friends slowly drifted apart to attend other churches.

One Sunday, my pastor spoke on "Remember to Keep the Sabbath Day Holy." So when my father asked me to buy him a

Sunday paper, I piously refused. "This is the Lord's Day and the newspaper is worldly. It isn't good for you spiritually." My dad became furious and hit me with his cane. He yelled, "I don't want anything to do with your crazy religion." I mistakenly rejoiced for getting persecuted, because I was certain that persecution for righteousness' sake would be greatly rewarded in heaven. I didn't understand that I was suffering for my foolishness.

Unwittingly, I was becoming legalistic and judgmental of others. I had developed a "holier than thou" attitude. I felt I was keeping all the rules by attending a Christian meeting somewhere every night of the week and five times on Sunday. But I was focusing on the wrong issues with my family and friends. I was neglecting the major issues of the Christian life such as showing grace, love and respect for others. Freedom to obey God's will is found in Christ. The liberation of His Spirit enables us to live sensible and well-rounded lives. The apostle Paul wrote in Second Corinthians 3:6, "[God] has made us competent as ministers of a new covenant—not of the letter but of the Spirit; for the letter kills, but the Spirit gives life."

While I did not trust good works to save my soul, I did erroneously believe that God's blessings were on me because I kept the rules set down by my church. I later discovered that true Christianity is much more than an academic belief system; it is a genuine relationship with the living God through Jesus our Lord. Walking together with God provides intimate fellowship with Him. It took me a number of years to appreciate fully that God's grace depends only on our relationship with Christ.

CHAPTER THREE

Spiritual Benefits for a Believer

Praise the LORD, O my soul,
and forget not all his benefits—
who forgives all your sins
and heals all your diseases,
who redeems your life from the pit
and crowns you with love and compassion.
(Psalm 103:2-4)

Salvation was only the first step of my spiritual journey. God had many additional blessings to bestow upon me. At my conversion, I knew for sure that all my sins were forgiven, but I was ignorant about the Holy Spirit. I wasn't familiar with the theological disputes about Him. If I had been, I might have resisted a wonderful encounter with the Holy Spirit of God.

Fighting over the terminology of spiritual experiences can be a waste of time and ruinous to relationships. I am glad that coming from a nonreligious Jewish home kept me in the dark about a lot of evangelical controversies. Before my conversion I never heard of consecration, sanctification, the baptism of the Spirit or even the filling of the Spirit. I wasn't even aware that the Holy Spirit existed, even though the Old Testament and the Jewish prayer book often speak of "the Spirit of God."

My ignorance of the Holy Spirit did not exclude me from the full blessings of God. A few days after I received Christ, I was walking on Lafayette Avenue toward Broadway. I was gratefully reflecting on the goodness of Jesus in saving me when something sudden and unexpected happened to me. In my mind's eye, I got a glimpse of heaven opening and the Spirit of God descending on me. Although I did not hear an audible voice, His introduction of Himself was clear to me, "I am the Holy Spirit and I have come to testify of Jesus." This was not another spirit; it was the same One who brought me to Jesus and assured me of forgiveness.

No one can cooperate with the Spirit of God unless he knows of His existence. We are commanded to walk in the Spirit, to be filled with the Spirit, to pray in the Spirit, not to grieve the Holy Spirit, not to quench the Spirit and not to resist the Spirit. We can only follow those biblical instructions by personally being acquainted with the Spirit. Recognizing my limitations, the Spirit revealed Himself to me in a unique way. The Holy Spirit endowed me with many benefits.

The Benefit of Spiritual Guidance

Many people wander aimlessly through life, muddling their way, making major decisions without a clue about what is best for them—what education to pursue, which person to marry, what career to choose or what religion to follow.

Life keeps changing on us. Each new phase of life forces us into new, unfamiliar territory. Just when we learn how to be children, we pop into adolescence, and when we find out how to cope as teenagers we are pushed into adulthood with all its responsibilities. We rapidly pass from being single adults into marriage, and then to being parents of little children who evolve into unpredictable teenagers. Before we are ready to let them go, they leave home to be on their own. Old age is upon us before we are prepared for it.

Time passes so quickly that it can be likened to getting up in the morning, admiring our youthful reflection in the mirror and then going into the kitchen to eat breakfast. Returning a short time later to get dressed, we look into the mirror and see the reflection of an old man. We wonder where the years went so quickly. Instead of talking about the march of time, we should speak about the rush of time. There is an old saying that goes, "Too soon old, too late smart."

Our greatest need in life is for a dependable guide, one who knows the way to take us from birth to eternity. Jesus promised us the very divine presence of God's Spirit as our companion and guide: "But the Counselor, the Holy Spirit, whom the Father will send in my name, will teach you all things " (John 14:26); "But when he, the Spirit of truth, comes, he will guide you into all truth" (16:13).

The Holy Spirit guided me when I didn't know what to do. Shortly after I became a believer, I felt an extreme hunger for God's Word. I wanted a Bible but did not have the money to buy one. I begged my pastor to give me a Bible. Finally he gave me an old discarded Bible with such tiny print that I could hardly read it. Yet it became a source of spiritual encouragement to me. Every day, God spoke to me through His written Word. I hid my Bible so that my father would not find it, tear it up and throw it out.

As a teenager and a new Christian I asked my heavenly Father to raise me. I believed that true manliness and spirituality could come only from God. I prayed, "Heavenly Father, please develop me into a real man, into a genuine Christian."

One day I faced a serious question I didn't know how to resolve. Was my earthly father still my father or did our relationship end when God became my heavenly Father? Did I still have to obey my unbelieving earthly father? The conflict came to a climax when my father asked me to come to the grocery store at 2 o'clock in the afternoon to help him carry the groceries home. Being alone in the house gave me the opportunity to read my Bible and commune with God without interference. As it got closer to the time to go, I was torn between wanting to stay home and read my Bible, which I preferred to do, and the fear of disobeying my dad. A number of times I walked to the door to go and help my father but then returned to the couch to read my Bible. I wondered what the right thing to do was. I needed to make a quick decision. How could I please my heavenly Father and my dad at the same time? Standing in the hallway, confused and uncertain, I cried out to God, "Father, I don't know what to do!"

For the first and only time in my life I heard God's audible voice, "Go thy way and help thy father." Not understanding King James language, I worried about the meaning of the words, "Go thy way." I foolishly wondered if God was sending me away from Him. I soon dismissed that unworthy doubt.

God still speaks to me, but not with an audible voice. I never heard His audible voice again, even though I sought for it many times. As we read His written Word we can hear Him speak to us in a personal way. He speaks with an inaudible but unmistakable voice. His directions can bypass our ears and penetrate our hearts.

Later, I told my pastor about my episode. After a moment of reflective silence, he said, "Well, that advice is according to Scripture, 'Honor thy father and mother.' So it must be of God." My pastor gave me a guiding principle for my life that I have followed ever since. It is a simple rule: God never contradicts Himself. If an experience, an inspirational idea or a new revelation is contrary to the moral, ethical or theological truth of the Bible, it is not from God.

I decided if God expected me to be an obedient son, I would do my very best to help my parents. Since my mother worked outside the home, I volunteered to clean the house, to shop for food and to make dinner for the family. One day my father gave my sisters their weekly allowance but decided not to give me any money. He claimed I would give it away to the church. I indignantly argued, "Dad, look at what I willingly do to help the family while Louise and Florence won't raise a finger to assist me." My father relented and gave me my allowance with a little extra. I maintained a good testimony with my parents by obeying God.

God speaks to us in different ways at different times. The Lord may speak through a Bible verse or by a gentle whisper of His Spirit within our minds. The Bible tells us in Isaiah 30:21: "Whether you turn to the right or to the left, your ears will hear a voice behind you, saying, 'This is the way; walk in it.' "

The Benefit of Spiritual Power

My encounter with the Spirit empowered me to persuade others to believe in Jesus. My pastor got tired of me pestering him to let me speak at our open-air meetings. I understand his reluctance. I was a sickly looking, poorly dressed fifteen-year-old kid. Finally, he gave me three minutes to share my testimony. I ended my talk with an invitation to accept Jesus. Eleven people raised their hands to accept Christ right there on the street corner! Whatever doubts my pastor had about the authenticity of my experience with the Holy Spirit vanished. My encounter with God's Spirit was biblically sound. Our resurrected Lord Jesus said to His disciples in Acts 1:8, "But you will receive power when the Holy Spirit comes on you; and you will be my witnesses in Jerusalem, and in all Judea and Samaria, and to the ends of the earth."

The Spirit of God also infused me with energy and spiritual zeal which motivated me to serve Him. From the day I was filled with the Holy Spirit, I was on the lookout for opportunities to witness about Jesus. More than anything else in my life, I ardently desired to win people to the Lord. I began by witnessing to my Jewish classmates while still in elementary school. They showed great interest in what I was saying. The principal called me into her office to speak to me about this.

She said, "Jewish parents are complaining about you telling their children about Jesus. It would be too bad if you could not graduate with your class." She warned me to stop witnessing about Jesus or she would be forced to take some serious steps to stop me. I was ready to suffer the consequences for Jesus, but my pastor advised me to submit to the principal, who was in authority over me. I hated myself for keeping silent, but I followed his counsel. In my zeal, I would rather have been a martyr for Jesus than a graduate of elementary school.

I kept looking in other places for opportunities to witness for Jesus. I asked a Jewish Mission for free tracts to distribute. "Of course," Dr. Cohen said, "and we will pay you 75 cents an hour to do it." It sounded good to me because I needed the money. I went to the nearest Jewish neighborhood and began giving out the literature. A number of young men threatened to beat me up. A sympathetic Jewish man restrained the irritated crowd. "Take it easy on him! Look, he is only a kid. I bet he is doing this just to make some extra money."

I would have liked to have been able to say, "I am not getting paid to give out this literature. I am doing this because I truly believe in Jesus." From then on, I refused to take money from the mission for giving out tracts.

While seeking for other opportunities to witness for the Lord, I heard about the Victory Center located in Times

Square. The Christian Businessmen during the Second World War operated it. Soldiers and sailors were on leave after their basic training. They were hoping for a good time before being sent overseas to the European warfront. We invited them in from the street for refreshments and an opportunity to hear the gospel. Many of them were away from home for the first time. They were lonely, homesick and fearful. Their tender hearts were ready for God. For weeks, I had the joy and excitement of leading many servicemen to Christ.

The new director of the center, a retired businessman, called me into the office. He told me, "I appreciate your desire to share Christ, but in my opinion, you are much too young to do personal evangelism at the center. We are looking for mature men to serve in that function." I tried to argue, but to no avail. I left disappointed but not discouraged. I thought, *Surely there must be other opportunities to win people to Christ.* I decided to look for them. The one characteristic that kept me from occasional discouragement was my simple trust in the Lord. No matter who misunderstood me, rejected me or opposed me, I knew that Jesus accepted me and kept me secure in His love.

The Benefit of Spiritual Discipline

Our heavenly Father doesn't want to do all our thinking for us, nor does He stop us from making mistakes. I have learned much more through my mistakes than through my successes. God's Spirit teaches and corrects us with loving discipline.

I experienced such an episode after an older Christian volunteered to disciple me. Since no one else showed that much interest in me, I was delighted. Unfortunately, my mentor was a chronic critic of others. He pointed out the faults of the congregation from the pastor on down. Up to that time I had loved going to church. My pastor was my hero. I enjoyed his messages until I found out he had purchased a television set. My teacher railed against him for bringing the world into his living room.

I was becoming just like my mentor. My smug self-righteousness gave me a lot of perverse pleasure, but it was also isolating me from the people of God. My critical spirit began to destroy my respect for the people who had accepted me with grace in spite of all my imperfections. My mentor, Willie, bragged about me, saying, "It is amazing that a fifteen-year-old boy like you has so much spiritual discernment." It felt good to believe in my spiritual superiority above all the other Christians I knew.

One evening while walking home from a session with Willie, I was reflecting on the sins and imperfections of other Christians. God interrupted my thoughts and emphatically spoke to me—not with an audible voice like He had done once before—but I got the message. "If you would spend as much time looking into your own heart as you try to look into the hearts of others, you would be a great Christian."

I felt His rebuke deeply. I apologized to the Lord and asked Him to help me overcome my critical attitude. Becoming positive wasn't easy for me because criticism had become a pleasant, addictive habit.

The Lord's rebuke did not discourage me. In a way I rejoiced to know that God cared enough to discipline me. If it were left up to my own imagination, my self-centered ego would have congratulated me for having such brilliant insights into the faults of others.

Not long after the rebuke, God started showing me all my faults and imperfections. For a while it wasn't any fun reading my Bible, because every time I opened the book, I had to face something else that was wrong with me. Submitting to discipline, even from a loving Father, isn't pleasant but it is necessary for our own good, as the Bible tells us.

> You have forgotten the exhortation which is addressed to you as sons,
>
> > "My son, do not regard lightly the discipline of the Lord, nor faint when you are reproved by Him; For those whom the Lord loves He disciplines, and He scourges every son whom He receives."
>
> It is for discipline that you endure; God deals with you as with sons; for what son is there whom his father does not discipline? (Hebrews 12:5-7, NASB)

Slowly, I began to understand that God overlooked my faults and imperfections when He accepted me into His family. He wanted me to do the same for others. Jesus knew exactly what He was getting when He accepted me in 1943. He wasn't under any illusions about me. As a teenage Christian, I thought by the time I became thirty, I would reach perfection. Although I am still maturing in Christ, I haven't yet attained the perfection I desire. Now that I am over seventy, I realize how dependent I am on the grace of God. John the beloved Apostle wrote in his old age, "If we claim to be without sin, we deceive ourselves and the truth is not in us. If we confess our sins, he is faithful and just and will forgive us our sins and purify us from all unrighteousness" (1 John 1:8-9).

The Holy Spirit is the Spirit of grace. Since God overlooks our serious faults, we should overlook the faults of others. Jesus, the only perfect Man who ever lived on this planet, forgave me, an imperfect sinner; therefore, I should be willing to forgive my fellow sinners.

The Benefit of Spiritual Wisdom

The Spirit of God who resides in us bestows wisdom, understanding and knowledge (see Isaiah 11:2). He also interacts with our thinking, emotions and behavior. I discovered early on in my Christian life that He feels my joy and pain, my gladness and sadness, my emotional ups and downs, even as I can feel His love and compassion, His grief or pleasure. The most unforgettable moments of my life were when God gave me the understanding of His heart.

After I found out how the ancient Jewish leaders mistreated Jesus, I told God that I was ashamed of being Jewish. Unexpectedly, I sensed the displeasure of God's Spirit with my way of thinking. I decided to study the issue of the crucifixion of Jesus. The Spirit of God became my Teacher once again. He showed me the false and unjust accusation against the Jewish people.

Whatever happened 2,000 years ago and whoever was responsible for the crucifixion of Jesus, the Bible tells us that one generation cannot be blamed or punished for the sins of another generation. When the mob outside Pilate's palace cried out, "Crucify him! . . . Let his blood be on us and on our children" (Matthew 27:22, 25), they had no legal right or authority to bring down a curse upon their children for their misdeeds. The Bible reveals the justice of God in an important statement found in Deuteronomy 24:16: "Fathers shall not be put to death for their children, nor children put to death for their fathers; each is to die for his own sin."

I then investigated the New Testament to discover what the historic record actually said about the betrayal of Jesus the Messiah. Luke 20:19 caught my attention. "The teachers of the law and the chief priests looked for a way to arrest him immediately, because they knew he had spoken this parable against them. But they were afraid of the people."

Some of the religious leaders, not the Jewish people, put together a secret plot against Jesus. In fact, the leaders had to execute their conspiracy in the middle of the night while Jerusalem was asleep. They rushed their plan through before the people could react and save Jesus. The reason they dragged Jesus to the Roman governor to be crucified was because they suspected that they could not win in an open trial under Jewish law. They also wanted the people to blame the Romans for the execution of Jesus, while they would pretend innocence. The leaders feared the people because they had regarded Jesus as the son of David and a prophet of God. When Jesus entered Jerusalem the people had received Him well. The historic record is found in Matthew 21:9: "The crowds that went ahead of him and those that followed shouted, 'Hosanna to the Son of David!' 'Blessed is he who comes in the name of the Lord!' 'Hosanna in the highest!' " "Hosanna" means "save us now." The people of Jerusalem were looking to Jesus as the Messiah to immediately save their nation politically. They were ready to make Him king.

Who then were the people who composed the mob outside Pilate's palace? It was the eve before the Passover celebration, when pious Jews came from all over the ancient world to worship at Jerusalem. They were susceptible to be incited against Jesus by the temple priests and teachers of the law. As strangers and pilgrims to Jerusalem, they did not know much about Jesus the Galilean. Who would God heed? Would God answer the shouts of an ignorant mob or the dying request of His Son, who cried out on the cross, "Father, forgive them, for they do not know what they are doing" (Luke 23:34)?

The answer is self-evident. God listened to the prayer of Jesus and answered it fifty days later during the feast of Pentecost. The Torah required Jewish men to worship God at Jerusalem three times a year: at Passover, Pentecost and the Feast of Tabernacles. Seven weeks after Passover, the same pious Jews who had cried out for the crucifixion of Jesus returned to Jerusalem to celebrate Pentecost. Acts 2:5, 14, 36-39 relates the historic episode.

> Now there were staying in Jerusalem God-fearing Jews from every nation under heaven. . . .
>
> Peter stood up with the Eleven, raised his voice and addressed the crowd. . . .
>
> "Therefore let all Israel be assured of this: God has made this Jesus, whom you crucified, both Lord and Christ."
>
> When the people heard this, they were cut to the heart and said to Peter and the other apostles, "Brothers, what shall we do?"
>
> Peter replied, "Repent and be baptized, every one of you, in the name of Jesus Christ for the forgiveness of your sins. And you will receive the gift of the Holy Spirit. The promise is for you and your children and for all who are far off—for all whom the Lord our God will call."

Peter was right to accuse those very people who stood before him of betraying their Messiah, because seven weeks prior at the Passover celebration in Jerusalem, they had been caught up in mob psychology, crying out for the blood of Jesus. During the interval between Passover and Pentecost, back home in their own countries, they had time to reflect on the injustice of their involvement in the death of an innocent victim. Three thousand of those guilty men heeded Peter and repented of their sin by placing their faith in Jesus. Returning to their home countries, they took the message of Jesus back with them and spread it all over the ancient world. Amazingly, the very people who had demanded His crucifixion laid down the very foundation of the Church.

It is unjust to accuse a contemporary Jew of crucifying Jesus, a crime initiated and committed by only a few Jewish leaders 2,000 years ago. Furthermore, the crucifixion of Jesus was God's eternal plan to reconcile this antagonistic world to Himself. Second Corinthians 5:18-19 explains this truth: "All this is from God, who reconciled us to himself through Christ and gave us the ministry of reconciliation: that God was reconciling the world to himself in Christ, not counting men's sins against them. And he has committed to us the message of reconciliation."

The infinite grace and love of God are beyond my understanding. God not only forgave those who were guilty of the blood of His Son, but He also adopted them into His Church. The Lord then used them to take the message of His love to the world.

God's Wisdom to Accept My Jewishness

Ashamed over my negative attitude and stupidity against my own people, I repented and apologized to Jesus, who loves His people, Israel. Jesus is not ashamed of being Jewish. He is still the Jewish Messiah and the anointed King of

Israel. I now rejoice that I am a Jew who follows Jesus, the true Messiah of Israel.

The Benefit of Spiritual Truth

After my conversion, my father suddenly became militantly Jewish. He dragged me to the rabbi to talk some sense to me. The rabbi's study, with his many diplomas on the wall, was very intimidating for me. Scholarly books were scattered everywhere. But he was a patient and kind man. He challenged me with two questions. First he asked me, "Where does it say in our Bible that God ever had a son?" He said that the idea that God has a son is a Gentile idea that came from pagan mythology and Christianity.

I pointed out Psalm 2:6-8 to him and asked him to translate it from the Hebrew text. He read,

> I have installed my King
> on Zion, my holy hill.
>
> I will proclaim the decree of the LORD:
>
> He said to me, "You are my Son;
> today I have become your Father.
> Ask of me,
> and I will make the nations your inheritance,
> the ends of the earth your possession.

The rabbi went on to his second question without replying to my question. "Where in our Bible is the Messiah ever called Jesus?" At the time, I could not answer him. I did not understand why the New Testament called the Messiah Jesus.

Then one day as I was studying the Hebrew word for salvation, "Yeshua," I read the angel's message to Joseph, "Thou shalt call his name JESUS: for he shall save his people from their sins" (Matthew 1:21, KJV). The light dawned on me: Jesus' Hebrew name is "Yeshua," which means "salvation"! The transliteration from the Hebrew to the Greek is "Jesus."

The Old Testament declares the Messiah's name as "Yeshua" in many passages. One is Isaiah 12:2-4:

> "Surely God is my salvation [my Yeshua, my Jesus];
> I will trust and not be afraid.
> The LORD, the LORD, is my strength and my song;
> he has become my salvation [my Yeshua, my Jesus]."
> With joy you will draw water
> from the wells of salvation [Yeshua].
>
> In that day you will say:
>
> "Give thanks to the LORD, call on his name [Yeshua];
> make known among the nations what he has done,
> and proclaim that his name is exalted."

One of my uncles was very angry with me about my conversion. He asked me, "How can you believe in Jesus when Christians did such terrible things to our family?"

I knew about the pogroms in Russia. On October 18, 1905, a week-long pogrom broke out in dozens of towns and villages throughout Russia. Hundreds of Jews were killed, thousands were wounded, and over 40,000 Jewish homes and shops were destroyed in the rioting, all done in the name of Jesus. The persecutions drove my family out of Russia.

I replied, "They misrepresented Jesus. He taught love and forgiveness even to one's enemies. They were false Christians. The reason I believe in Jesus is because I have discovered that He is the true Messiah, the hope of Israel. The only way I can truly be Jewish in God's eyes is to believe in His Son, Jesus." My uncle gave up trying to dissuade me from my faith.

Much later in life, I discovered that Rabbinic Judaism is based on a faulty premise. Their presumption is that God gave to Israel two laws on Mount Sinai, a written law and an oral law. The oral law was passed down for over 1,000 years from mouth to mouth. In 200 A.D. Rabbi Yehudah Ha Nasi had gathered all the oral laws and written them down in a book called the *Mishna*. This was the foundation of the Talmud, whose commentaries took centuries to complete. Moses commanded Israel in Deuteronomy 12:32: "See that you do all I command you; do not add to it or take away from it." Isaiah the Jewish prophet also spoke against creating man-made, traditional rules: "Their worship of me is made up only of rules taught by men" (Isaiah 29:13).

The Lord Jesus also spoke of the same danger: "In vain they worship Me, teaching as doctrines the commandments of men" (Mark 7:7, NKJV). The only law that God ever gave to Israel was the written Torah.

CHAPTER FOUR

Walking the Streets with God

For this God is our God for ever and ever;
he will be our guide even to the end.
(Psalm 48:14)

The Protection of Jesus

My spiritual birthday was sometime at the end of May in 1943. During my summer vacation, I wanted a job to make some money. New York State required children less than fifteen years of age to obtain a work permit for a summer job. I was required to take a physical examination to obtain my working papers. When the doctor who examined me heard my asthmatic breathing, he turned me down flat.

All summer long I spent my time walking the streets to get out of the house. I learned that the Lord was walking with me and protecting me.

Every Sunday evening, I attended the Bergen Street Alliance Tabernacle, which was two miles away from my house. The walk took me through a high-crime area, so I usually took a trolley car for personal safety. One evening, I had only a nickel, just enough for a one-way trip on the trolley, I decided to walk to church and use my money to ride home. On my way, two older teenagers stopped me. One said in a threatening voice, "Lend us a nickel, boy!"

I replied, "Do you want to take the Lord's money?"

The other boy said to his companion, "I ain't going to fool with no religious fellow."

They started to walk away, and I shouted, "Remember, Jesus loves you! Trust Him and He will save you!"

Since I told them it was the Lord's money, I felt compelled to put my nickel in the offering plate and trust the Lord to protect me on my walk back home through that crime-infested neighborhood.

The Healing Touch of Jesus

The Lord was not only protecting me while I was walking the streets, but He was also listening to me. One day while walking on Atlantic Avenue, I spoke my heart to God: "Lord, I have nothing to offer you in this life. My asthma is so severe and my eyesight is so poor that I can't obtain a working permit for a summer job. Besides, who would hire me? I can't do Your kingdom much good either. The only future I see for myself is on state welfare. Here is my solution to spare both You and me from a lot of humiliation: take me home to heaven right now and save me years of embarrassment and frustration."

The Lord whispered into my heart, "I want to show you what I can do with your life."

Not long after that dialogue with my Lord, my pastor used an illustration of D.L. Moody in one of his sermons. He had also been a school dropout with little hope for a productive life. He heard an evangelist say, "The world has yet to see what God can do through a person fully committed to Him." Moody said, "I want to be that man." God raised him up as a great evangelist who influenced over a million people to become Christians long before the invention of radio and television. After hearing the message that night, I also told God, "I want to be that man." I don't remember ever having a clear call to the ministry, but I did volunteer. I said to God, "Lord, you have called intelligent and personable people into Your full-time service that could do great things for You, and they have not accepted. I want to volunteer to take one of their places of service."

I gladly presented my sickly body to be a living sacrifice to God. At the altar, I laughed at myself for such a pathetic offering. I couldn't imagine why God would even want it. My ill health and poor vision could have prevented me from a full-time ministry, but I had no idea what God was about to do for me. One evening, while waiting for my turn to speak at a gospel street meeting, a stranger came over to me. He said, "I can hear you wheezing down the block. You are too sick to be out here." My chest was congested and felt very heavy, but I wasn't going to let that hinder me from sharing Jesus. He then asked me a penetrating question; "Do you believe God can heal you?"

I had never thought of it before, but I did believe God could do anything. So I said, "Yes! I do!"

He told me, "I am going to an Alliance church where the elders anoint the sick, and their prayer of faith brings healing to the sick. Come to my house, and I will anoint you with oil."

My new friend didn't do it exactly right. He wasn't an elder of a church, and when he didn't find any olive oil in his kitchen, he anointed me with castor oil. Amazingly, my wheezing stopped and all my allergies vanished. For the first time in my memory, my breathing was effortless. That night I enjoyed an uninterrupted sleep.

A month later, I told my mother that Jesus healed me.

She replied, "You just outgrew it."

"Mother, a few weeks ago, I wheezed every day. In one moment all my allergies were gone."

My mother shrugged her shoulders, threw her arms in the air and walked away without a word.

The Wisdom of Jesus

It is good that God does not always answer our prayers positively, because He knows what is best for us. Right after God healed me of asthma, I heard preachers say to their congregations, "If you have the faith, throw away your glasses and believe Him for perfect vision."

Since I had the faith, I threw away my eyeglasses. I testified at every opportunity that God had healed my vision. Sure, I still had the symptoms of poor vision, but I insisted the condition was healed and believed that in a short time I would see perfectly. For the next six months, I kept getting lost in the subway by taking the wrong trains. More than once I wanted to go to Brooklyn but I took the wrong train and ended up in the Bronx.

I could not deny it any longer; God hadn't healed my eyes. I did not understand why God did not do it for me, but I determined not to lose my trust in Him. I felt badly because a dear Christian lady had bought me the glasses that I had thrown away. I had to appear in public with my new pair of glasses. Humiliated and feeling like a total spiritual failure, I struggled with serious self-doubts. *If I had waited just another week or even a day more, maybe the miracle would have happened,* I told myself. The whole sorry episode challenged my faith and confidence in God, but I determined to trust Him anyway.

A few years later, I realized God did a good thing by not healing my vision. My life would have taken a much different direction if I had normal vision. When I reached my seventeenth birthday, I tried to join the army, the navy and even the marines all in the same day. In every case, I failed the eye test. I wrote a letter to President Truman, asking for his help to get into the army. A few weeks later a letter came from a commander of the infantry. The letter stated that if I still desired to join the army on my eighteenth birthday, I should report for immediate induction. However, the infantry did not appeal to me.

I thank God for not healing my eyesight at the age of seventeen because of His better plan for my life. I have learned that God not only shows His love by answering our prayers, but also by denying them. Our heavenly Father knows what is best for us.

After completing my first year of high school and failing every subject, my school counselor asked me what I wanted to do in life. I replied, "I want to be a pastor."

She looked at me very sadly and said, "It is too bad, but not every good guy finishes first in life." She was sympathetic but doubted that I would ever make it.

As a young Christian, I listened to many inspirational preachers who were doing great things for God and I longed to become a pastor. Understanding my human frailties and lack of ability, I explained to God in one of our chats, "Lord, I can never go into the ministry because I am not worthy to baptize anyone."

The Lord replied, "If only perfect people were allowed to baptize, no one would ever be baptized."

The apostle Paul wrote in Romans 15:15-16 that God's calling into the ministry is by grace alone and not by our merit. "Because of the grace that is given to me of God, that I should be the minister of Jesus Christ . . . ministering the gospel of God . . ." (KJV).

Quite often as I read the Bible, God turns His written Word into a personal message for me. The Spirit, who is the Author of those words, made them mine. While I was worrying about my future, I opened my Bible one day to this promise from Jeremiah 29:11-14:

> "For I know the plans I have for you," declares the LORD, "plans to prosper you and not to harm you, plans to give you hope and a future. Then you will call upon me and come and pray to me, and I will listen to you. You will seek me and find me when you seek me with all your heart. I will be found by you," declares the LORD.

I knew from that moment on that God had a special plan for my life, so I sought for it with all my heart and ultimately found it.

My first concern after flunking out of high school was getting a job. I finally found one at a candy factory. The owner invited me to eat all the chocolates I desired free of charge. I felt like I had gone to heaven, but after devouring chocolates for a couple of weeks, I lost my appetite for them and the very thought of chocolates made me sick to my stomach.

The owner had discovered that polishing cheap chocolates made them look like rich and expensive chocolates, which made higher profits. I became the official chocolate polisher. One day as I was polishing the chocolates I had come to hate, I felt some despair. I thought, *Is this all I can look forward to in my life—just being a chocolate polisher? How boring! How unproductive! What a dead-end job!*

God then spoke to me again in His inaudible but unmistakable voice, "You can't serve Me without an education." I realized that whatever career I followed in the future, I needed an education.

I replied, "Lord, You know how dumb I am. I was kept back in the fifth grade, and I failed all of my high school subjects. But I believe that You can open the door for me to return to school. If You do, I will go through it. I will do my very best; however, if I fail because of my inability, forgive me. I promise never to quit no matter how hard it gets for me."

The Reliability of Jesus

My first step was to apply to the Missionary Training Institute in Nyack, New York. My letter left a lot to be desired as far as spelling and grammar were concerned. A few weeks later their negative reply arrived. The letter read, "You must return to high school and get your diploma before we will consider your application." I said to the Lord, "I tried, but the door is closed."

That summer I attended an Alliance youth retreat at Nyack, New York. Harry Post, a missionary from Borneo, was the missionary speaker. As I listened to him, my desire to serve Christ intensified in my heart. At the end of the service, I caught him at the door and shared my situation with him. He replied, "I just came from a conference at Toccoa Falls Institute. They have a high school for students just like you, and also a Bible institute." He wrote out the address for me. As soon as I returned home, I applied to the Toccoa Falls High School. To my delight, I was accepted. I wondered what to do next.

God gave me guidance through a Christian friend. "Go on faith," he challenged me.

"What does that mean?" I asked.

"Either God's people will support you, or God will supply a job for you to work your way through school."

"That's good enough for me," I said.

I followed his advice and told everyone I was going to school by faith. One man gave me two old metal suitcases he had planned to throw away. The ladies of my church held a shower for me. They gave me sheets, blankets and curtains for my dormitory windows. But some well-intentioned people tried to discourage me from going back to school. A friend told me that Christ was coming back within five years. I could do more for the kingdom of God to stay home and give out tracts rather than wasting my time getting an education. He gave me that advice in 1945.

No one had fewer possibilities for success than I did. A friend of my father warned me, "You are making the biggest mistake of your life. In six months, you will return home like a beaten dog with his tail between his legs. You will fail because you don't have the ability to succeed. Stay home and I will hire you to be my stock boy; at least you will have some job security."

Since he wasn't a Christian and did not understand that God was leading me, I ignored his advice. Within six months, the corporation he worked for closed down his grocery store and he lost his managerial job. From that I learned that there is no guaranteed security in this world. I found my security in following Jesus. I am glad I followed the Lord's leading instead of listening to others.

My plan was to take the Greyhound bus to Georgia on a Monday morning in order to arrive on time for school. I didn't have any money for the bus ticket or for my education, but I believed the Lord would provide the money I needed. The night before I planned to leave for school I attended the evening service at my church. The pastor surprised me by calling me up to the platform to have the elders pray for me. The elders prayed for me, and the pastor had the congregation sing a hymn for me, "God Will Take Care of You."

> All you may need He will provide, God will take
> care of you;
> Nothing you ask will be denied, God will take
> care of you.
>
> No matter what may be the test, God will take
> care of you;
> Lean, weary one, upon His breast, God will take
> care of you.
>
> God will take care of you, through every day, O'er
> all the way;
> He will take care of you; God will take care of
> you.[1]

Then the pastor told the congregation he was going to take up a second offering. "I have never done this before," he said. "I don't have the time to get the approval of the elders, but God has told me to take up an offering to help Albert go to school." I received $60, enough money to purchase a one-way bus ticket to Toccoa, Georgia and to pay for the first month's room, board and tuition.

What I lacked in brainpower, I had in faith power. I believed in God's reliability and ability to fulfill His will for my life, no matter how impossible it seemed to me.

Note

1. Civilla D. Martin, "God Will Take Care of You," *Hymns of the Christian Life* (Camp Hill, PA: Christian Publications, 1978), #352.

CHAPTER FIVE

My Faith Adventure

But now, this is what the LORD says–
he who created you, O Jacob,
he who formed you, O Israel:
"Fear not, for I have redeemed you;
I have summoned you by name; you are mine.
When you pass through the waters,
I will be with you;
and when you pass through the rivers,
they will not sweep over you.
When you walk through the fire,
you will not be burned;
the flames will not set you ablaze.
For I am the LORD, your God,
the Holy One of Israel, your Savior;
I give Egypt for your ransom,
Cush and Seba in your stead."
(Isaiah 43:1-3)

Trusting Jesus Is Never a Mistake

Early Monday morning at 4:30, I left for the Greyhound Bus Terminal on 34th Street in Manhattan to take a bus to Georgia. My mother was too upset to say good-bye to me. She lamented, "I have lost my son."

I had never traveled outside of New York before. My bus trip took thirty-six long, weary and boring hours. I had very little understanding of the vastness and diversity of America. I also had a lot to learn about the injustices of this world. After we left Washington D.C., I could not believe the nerve and rudeness of the bus driver ordering all the African-Americans to move to the back of the bus. I was sure someone was going to punch him out or at least report him for insulting paying customers.

When I arrived in Toccoa, someone from the institute was at the bus station waiting for new students to arrive. He drove us two miles outside Toccoa to the school. After registration, I was taken to my dormitory room. A few minutes later, the dinner bell rang and a new friend and I found our way to the dining hall. For the first time I ate black-eyed peas, cornbread and turnip greens. (We were poor in Brooklyn, but we never ate the tops of turnips. We threw them away!) After dinner, I was getting acquainted with other students when the chapel bell rang. The superintendent of the school gave his orientation speech: "Remember, students, you make the record; we just keep it. In the future when someone calls us for a recommendation, I will go to your file and read it to him, so it had better be good for your own sake."

After the lecture was finished, I stayed to talk to a former pastor of my Brooklyn church. Everyone quickly left the chapel to return to their dormitories, leaving me behind.

I had no idea how to get back to my dormitory, nor was anyone in sight to give me directions. The sun had gone down and there were no streetlights. I had never been alone on a country road at night. My night sight was very limited. I looked out through the opened back doors of the auditorium and saw the lights of a building in the distance. It looked like my dorm, so I started down a hill toward the lights. Before I knew what was happening, I was falling off the wooden bridge without railings. Thinking quickly, I prayed, "Oh Lord, I hope there's water down there." Then in a flash, I remembered I couldn't swim.

My guardian angel was on duty that night. I had a strange weightless sensation of floating down in slow motion. I landed without a bruise in a muddy creek. A student had seen me stumble off the bridge. He helped me out of the creek and led me by the hand to my dorm. The red mud permanently stained and ruined my only sport jacket. Everyone on the campus heard of my misfortune, and I was humiliated. What else was waiting for me on my adventure of faith?

Amazingly, God touched my intellect and I was able to understand my lessons—it was as if a lightbulb was turned on in my brain. Six weeks later my report card came out. My first grading period was a success; I had better than passing grades for all my subjects. Even being an average student was light years away from what I had been.

Every day I went to my mailbox, hoping for a check to enable me to pay for my expenses at the institute, but none ever came. I had to go to plan B, which meant finding a job to earn my way through school. I unsuccessfully looked for a job in town. I made an appointment to see Kelly Barnes, the principal of the high school. I explained my plight and asked him for a job.

"Sorry," Dr. Barnes replied. "We have no work scholarships available. They've all been given out."

"So what should I do?" I asked.

"You should go home," he advised me.

"I don't want to."

"Why not?"

"Well, I am a Hebrew Christian." I don't know why I introduced myself that way; the words just came out without any forethought.

Dr. Kelly Barnes stood to his feet in excitement and said, "You don't have to say any more. Last night I was especially tired, but as I was falling asleep, a Bible verse woke me up. 'I will bless them that bless you.' I turned over and started to fall asleep again. The same verse woke me up again and again. I thought I was losing my mind, but now I know that God was preparing me for this meeting. If I bless you—a Jew—God will bless me."

Down on the Farm

He took me to the school's farm in his red Ford and left me in the barnyard in the care of a farm boy. The atmosphere smelled foul and my shoes were ruined in the cow muck. The first live cow I ever saw up close looked ferocious and dangerous to me. I asked the boy who was supposed to help me, "What am I supposed to do here?"

"Y'all supposed to milk the cows."

"How do I milk a cow?" I inquired.

"Y'all pump the cow's tail."

He seemed sincerely helpful. He put a milk pail under the right place, handed me the tail of the cow and instructed me on how to pump the tail to get the most milk from the cow.

I said, "But I am not getting anything."

"Well, you have to pull harder," he retorted. But still no milk came, and the cow seemed annoyed.

Just then the head farmer came in and asked me, "Young man, what are you doing?"

"I'm milking the cow."

He told me that I was a menace to myself and sent me back to Kelly Barnes with a note telling him the story. Kelly almost fell to the floor, laughing and crying all at the same time. "Well," he said, "God knew you needed a lot of help. Now I am sure of a double blessing."

Off we went again in his red Ford. This time he took me to the kitchen and left me in the care of two hefty cooks. They had 150 live chickens to be prepared for dinner. They took me outside along with the live chickens to a tree stump. A fire was already set and over it stood a large cooking pot of boiling water. They handed me an ax and explained how to grab a live chicken by its neck, place it on the stump and chop off its head. Then I was to grab the headless chicken by its claws and dip it into the boiling water, which would loosen its feathers, making it easy to pluck them out. The cooks explained how to cut the chickens up into pieces for the frying pan and then they left me alone to finish my task.

I had never killed anything before. I nervously took the first chicken by the neck and placed its head on the stump. The chicken looked up at me pitifully as if to say, "Please, mister, don't hurt me." I thought, *It's either you or my job.* I chopped off its head, but to my surprise it didn't die. The headless chicken kept kicking and jerking. I threw it down and yelled at it, "In the name of the Lord, come out of that chicken." The cooks heard me and came running to see what the commotion was all about. When I explained, they broke out into hysterical laughter. They supervised as I killed all the rest of the chickens. The more chickens I killed, the easier it became.

I had a lot to learn about living in the country away from city conveniences. The school decided to build a dam above the Toccoa Falls. The land had to be free of undergrowth. Dr. Barnes picked me up in his red Ford and drove me to the area that had to be cleared. He handed me an ax and left me with a country boy to supervise me. For every tree I chipped away at he cut down four trees.

But I was getting to like being in the woods. It was invigorating to smell the fresh air with a scent of pine needles. The quiet, with the occasional songs of the birds, became very enjoyable. One day after chopping down a tree, I came upon a trickle of spring water dripping out of a hillside. It formed a small pool of water. I had never before or since ever drunk such deliciously pure water. Several times each day I satisfied my thirst at the spring.

One hot afternoon, I approached the spring with a dry thirst and my empty cup. A long black snake cooling itself in the pool of water caught me by surprise. It saw me before I saw it. The snake sprung at me, missing me by a hair. When I described the snake to my country friends, they thought it was likely a poisonous water moccasin snake. I knew that the angel of the Lord was watching over me. After this experience, I lost my sense of security in the woods. I requested a different job on the safety of the campus.

I was assigned to another work supervisor. Eager to win her approval, I worked quickly to finish the list of tasks she gave me. I kept asking her for more and more work to impress her with my diligence. Instead of praise, she criticized, "Runge, you never seem to have enough work to do."

Whenever she caught a glimpse of me passing by her office window, she assumed I was idle and needed something else to do. She shouted across the campus, "Runge, we've got a job for you." I was supposed to work only thirty-five hours a week, but I was doing fifty hours a week. I talked to Kelly Barnes about the pressure my supervisor was putting me under.

"Use diplomacy," he suggested. Thinking his words over, I got the idea to look busy all the time. I took a big monkey wrench with me wherever I went, to my classes, to meals, even to my dormitory. When my supervisor saw me walking at a fast pace around the campus, swinging a monkey wrench, she assumed I was busy on a job. She never called on me again to do extra jobs for her. She even congratulated me for improving my work skills.

My next job assignment was taking care of the furnaces on the campus. Kelly Barnes confided in me that the financial resources of the school were in bad shape. All he could afford was one boxcar of coal that had to last us the rest of the winter. I was instructed to close the furnaces down from 9 p.m. to 5 a.m. I was not to tell anyone about the situation.

Most people were satisfied except my work supervisor and the Dean of Women, who resided in the girl's dorm. They insisted on more heat than my allotted coal supply allowed. They complained and fussed so much that I got sick of it and decided to leave school and join the army. The two ladies smiled and said, "Good idea, Runge."

As I sat in the army enlistment center waiting to enlist, I remembered my promise to God never to quit no matter how hard it got. I walked the two miles back to school to eat humble pie. The two ladies were not pleased to see me again.

Kelly Barnes decided to save me from the wrath of those women by giving me another job. I turned the furnaces over to the practical joker who had told me to pump a cow's tail to get milk. The women ecstatically exclaimed to everyone, "Now that we have Runge off the job, we will get some heat." Unfortunately, the first night on the job, the farm boy forgot to turn the water on and blew up the furnace. It took a year and a half for the school to replace the furnace for the girl's dorm. Kelly Barnes enjoyed telling my adversaries, "What did I tell you? God's Word says, 'I will curse them that curse you.' You better be careful how you treat that Hebrew boy, Runge."

I was born with comedian genes and a keen sense of Jewish humor. On one occasion, I got a part in a school drama. I was supposed to portray a mean-spirited and unforgiving father. The director covered my hair with makeup making me look bald. The moment I stepped out on stage, the audience of my fellow students broke out in roars of laughter. What was meant to be a tragic drama became a comedy of errors. The plot was about a wayward daughter who ran away from home and had an illicit affair and an illegitimate child. Homeless, penniless and desperate, she and her baby made their way through a blizzard back to her parents' home. On the doorstep she begged for forgiveness and the help of her father.

I stood blocking the doorway. I was supposed to send her away with angry words. It all seemed so out of character for me that I was unable to stifle my snickering long enough to keep a stern face. I tried to say, "Go away and never come back," but I was laughing too hard to say anything. Everyone broke out in uncontrollable laughter. I could not go on. The curtains came down. I got scolded for ruining the play and my understudy took over. My teacher was infuriated, but the students thought it was the best show they had ever seen. I was never given another major part in a school play.

Jesus Overrides Our Mistakes

Expecting to be able to make money in Brooklyn during the summer months, I returned home seeking a job. But no one wanted to hire me just for the summer. Someone suggested I lie and say I was looking for a full-time job. I refused because I did not believe in lying. I trusted God to provide for me.

Although I searched diligently, nothing was available except as a camp counselor at Pinebrook Camp for boys. Room and board were provided along with $10 a week for spending money. I did not earn enough money to return to Toccoa Falls to finish my senior year of high school. I found a small unaccredited Bible school in Atlanta, Georgia that would accept me without a down payment or a high school diploma. I hitchhiked to Georgia. To be fair, I felt obligated to stop at Toccoa to explain to Dr. R.A. Forrest my reason for not coming back to complete my course. He seemed very sympathetic, but informed me that the school was in a grave financial crisis. "We may have to close down before the end of this semester. The town merchants now require us to pay cash in advance. We have lost our credit standing in the community."

He just sat there reflecting silently for what seemed a long time. Neither of us said a word. He broke the silence by inviting me to stay that night as his guest so he could pray about it. In my heart, I really wanted to return to Toccoa and finish high school.

I didn't sleep much that night. Early the next day, I nervously waited for Dr. Forrest to arrive at his office. At last he showed up and called me into his office. "Runge," he said, smiling, "God has told me you should finish your high school education here. Once you get your diploma, you can go on to higher education. I don't know how we will survive financially, but God is able. If we go down, we will go down together."

The story of how God worked it all out is amazing. In Toccoa there was a poorly dressed man who lived in a broken-down shack. Most people thought he was penniless. They all looked down on him—except for Dr. Forrest. He always had a kind word and a cheerful greeting for him. Unbeknownst to everyone in town, that poor man wasn't so poor after all. He died and left all his money to Dr. Forrest and Toccoa Falls Institute. In his will he had written, "Dr. Forrest is the only person who ever treated me with respect." God not only saved the school, but also enabled me to finish high school.

On graduation day no one from Brooklyn was there to celebrate my achievement. There were no congratulatory cards from anyone back home. I watched all my friends leaving the campus after the ceremony with their parents for a special dinner at a restaurant in town. No one invited me along to celebrate. The campus dining room was closed for the evening meal, so I sat alone in my dormitory room with a cold can of beans for dinner.

Feeling sorry for myself, I suddenly became aware of the presence of the Lord. Although I could not see Him, His love and approval warmed my heart. We celebrated together. As I write these words, I am weeping tears of love and appreciation for the memory of that precious experience.

Jesus Ever Leads Us to Make Right Decisions

After finishing my secondary education, I entered the Toccoa Falls Bible College. Toward the end of my freshman year, I got word that my father was very ill and not expected to live long. During the last few years of his life, my dad practically lived at the veteran's hospital. I hitchhiked home from Georgia to see my dad for what was to be the last time.

I was pleased to find my dad feeling better and out of bed. A changed man stood before me. There was sadness in his eyes; he spoke with a soft voice, "Before we say good-bye, I want to show you something important to both of us."

With a shaky hand, he pulled a small blue book from the pocket of his bathrobe. It was a prophecy edition of the New Testament. I was speechless. Standing before me was my inflexible dad, the atheist, the cynic, the critic, the man who had torn up all my Christian tracts while angrily shouting at me, "You have disgraced the family's name with your Christianity!" The impossible had happened. My dad now believed in Jesus!

All my resentments against him for never hugging me, for never taking me to a ball game, for never saying he loved me, for never affirming me, for fighting my faith, melted away by the grace of God. I had given up all hope for my dad's conversion. Little did I suspect how much my heavenly Father loved him!

When I returned home with a slight Georgia drawl, my Yiddish mother said, "Vhat? You don't speak English no more." She dreamt that I had entered a monastery where they had shaved off all my hair and the monks mistreated me because I was Jewish. When my mother saw my premature balding, she was convinced that her worst fears were true. I was not able to convince her that my evangelical Bible school was not a monastery. She had no idea of the great love and friendship I had found at Toccoa Falls Institute. Toccoa Falls was more than a school for me. It was my family. I could never repay the great debt I owe to those beloved people of Toccoa Falls High School and College. I will always appreciate the love and acceptance I received there.

I applied to Nyack College, the very school that had rejected my original application until I had finished high school. I was accepted as a transfer student from Toccoa Falls. I am not fully sure why I left to attend Nyack College. Maybe because it was the year my father died. Maybe I left because the work scholarship students were now required to pay $10 a month in addition to their thirty-five hours of work a week and I could not imagine where I would get that money. I accumulated what at that time seemed like an enormous school debt of $160. Maybe it was that I had grown up and felt the need of leaving my school family to go out on my own. Most likely it was for all those reasons.

I wanted to go to summer school for a head start on the fall semester. After attending an evening service in my Brooklyn church, a couple invited me to come to their home for refreshments. They had something they wanted to tell me. "We have sold our home for a profit," they told me. "We want to put our tithe toward your education at Nyack." They gave me enough to complete summer school.

Before the fall term began, Mr. Donald Ebner, the treasurer of the Gospel Meeting House, called me into his office. He took out his checkbook and asked me how much I needed to begin my fall term. I was hesitant to say but he was insistent. I told him I needed $180 to begin the semester. Without blinking an eye, he wrote out the check for the complete amount and gave it to me.

In order to pay for the entire semester, I needed a job. My first was as a house painter. Everything was going well until my boss told me to paint the outside window frame on the third floor. To do it, I had to climb an outside ladder up to the third story to get to the window. Holding a paint can in one hand and the brush with the other hand, I looked up and saw how high up I had to climb to get to the window frame. My legs froze and stuck to the ground. They had a mind of their own. They refused to get on the first rung of the ladder. There was nothing I could do to even take the first step. My boss told me to climb the ladder or I would be fired. You can guess what happened. I walked back to the campus feeling like a failure, but the Holy Spirit comforted me. I knew I had done my best.

I did better at my second job at a box factory. I worked three days a week from 3 o'clock in the afternoon to midnight. I gave it my best, but the union steward came over to me and told me to slow down my productivity, because it made the other workers look bad.

Nyack College was a good experience for me, even though I had a few embarrassing experiences. In my homiletic class I gave my first sermon. I had learned to preach in the South, where emotional exhortations were encouraged. I gave it all I had. I worked up a sweat. I shouted as I banged the pulpit more than once to emphasize my main points. Finally, I concluded my talk and sat down, expecting a lot of praise for speaking so powerfully. With an expressionless face, my professor looked at me and said in front of the class, "Mr. Runge, we are not training tobacco auctioneers here at Nyack."

For a full week, I could hardly lift my head until I received a consoling letter from my professor, explaining what was behind his criticism. He wrote, "What we say is more important than how we say it. Think through your content more carefully." Although I didn't lose my fire to preach, I began to pay more attention to what I said in my sermons.

I wanted to sing solos. While at Nyack, I decided to pay for voice lessons. My voice teacher worked hard with me, but finally she had to tell me, "Mr. Runge, you have a very unusual talent."

"Really," I replied. "Tell me more."

"Well, you are the only student I have ever had that can change keys ten times in the same song and never know it."

Her honest appraisal ended my singing career before it began. The only subject I failed after returning to school was music appreciation.

Jesus Uses Our Disappointments to Redirect Us

The vast majority of Christians who have touched my life were honorable people whom I came to rely on and trust. I was unprepared for a professing Christian who did not or could not keep his promises. The director of a Messianic Center recruited me to do missionary work for the summer. He promised me enough money to return to Bible school for my senior year. At the end of the summer, however, he apologized, saying that he did not have the money. He blamed his board for refusing to support his promise. I lost an entire school semester. Obviously there was some kind of communication breakdown.

I found a job selling men's clothes at Goldsmith Department Store for the Christmas holidays. I did so well at selling clothes that I was given a "permanent" job selling cameras. I did not even know how to put film in a camera. My job was short-lived.

My mother was overjoyed, thinking that I had forsaken my pursuit for the Christian ministry. About that time I heard of a faith mission that planned to send people to Israel for a two-year term to distribute gospel literature. My friends were very willing to help me on my way to the mission field. I was at a crossroads. Should I finish my education or go to Israel? I was reminded of God's challenge that I could not serve Him without an education and of my promise not to quit school no matter how difficult it became. It was a hard decision because I had already told everyone I was going overseas. They were disappointed with my decision to pursue my education.

My educational opportunity looked bleak, but in my darkest moments God always came through for me. One day Miss Hilda Koser, a missionary from the American Board of

Missions to the Jews, found me working behind a sales counter.

She told me, "Albert, Dr. Cohn has been looking for you. Go to his office."

On my day off, I took the subway to Manhattan and walked a block to his office. As I was crossing Broadway at 72nd Street to get to the mission's headquarters, my legs suddenly felt so heavy I couldn't move another inch. Before I could blink an eye, a speeding truck raced by me right through the red light. I had not seen him coming. I was within an inch of getting hit. Less than a step more and I would have been history! A traffic cop ran over to me, expecting to see me dead. Excitedly he said, "I was sure you were hit by that truck! I can't believe you are alive!"

I once heard my pastor say, "The safest place to be is in the center of God's will for your life." The Bible tells us in Psalm 34:7: "The angel of the LORD encamps around those who fear him, and he delivers them."

"I am sorry to disappoint you," I said to the traffic cop with a brave grin and shaking knees. The angel of the Lord was taking care of me that day.

When I finally reached his office, Dr. Cohn told me, "Albert, Miss Sussdorf begged me to give you one of our scholarships. I refused, telling her, 'We might as well throw the money in the East River. Albert will never amount to anything,' but God has shown me that I was wrong. Apply to Houghton College and the Mission will pay all your expenses."

God turned my disappointment into His appointment. I never expected to be able to go to a Christian liberal arts college. All my previous academic work from Toccoa Falls and Nyack College was accepted with full credit.

Houghton College challenged me academically. The professors were not only deeply committed to God, but they were also professionally well trained. Whether I studied philosophy, psychology, literature, Latin, German, botany, zoology or Bible, all my professors had earned doctorates in their chosen fields. Every class was interesting and challenging. While at Houghton, I had an intellectual awakening. I became analytical; I learned to question my assumptions and to think through my beliefs. It was while at Houghton that I committed myself to a lifetime of learning. Even now in my seventies, my prayer is, "Lord, give me the curiosity of a child and the wisdom of an adult."

One of the best compliments paid to me while at Houghton was from a professor who told me, "Mr. Runge, you are an overachiever," meaning I accomplished things beyond my ability. He was right, but I wasn't working alone. The Lord Jesus was helping me.

CHAPTER SIX

Finding My Soulmate

A wife of noble character who can find?
She is worth far more than rubies.
(Proverbs 31:10)

Right after I became a Christian, I prayed, "Lord, I want you to choose my wife for me." I was fifteen at the time, living in Brooklyn, while my future wife was ten years old growing up in Amsterdam, New York.

The Lord spoke to me at the beginning of the fall semester of my senior year, "The woman you will marry is now on campus."

I kept looking for her. This wasn't necessary because the Lord had it all planned out. We met returning from a senior-sophomore picnic. Lee was standing behind me in line as we were waiting to board the bus back to the campus. She was a transfer student from Buffalo State University, where she took art education on an art scholarship. She transferred in her sophomore year because she desired to go to a Christian school. Without having requested a catalog and an application from Houghton College, they arrived in the mail. Lee took it as guidance from the Lord.

Her parents weren't very happy that she gave up her art scholarship, which paid her way fully to Buffalo State University, to go to another college. Lee promised them that she would work her way through school if necessary. When they realized she was determined, they reluctantly gave their consent.

While we were waiting for the bus to return us to the campus, I spoke to her about Bible prophecy on various subjects such as the antichrist, the Great Tribulation and the Abomination that causes desolation. I sensed she was impressed with my biblical knowledge. Lee was a new Christian from a liberal church, and she had never heard of Bible prophecy before. She hadn't told me her name or where she resided at school. I kept looking for her on campus, but she was nowhere to be found. One afternoon while walking in the hallway of the classroom building, I suddenly felt very faint and sat down to rest. A few minutes later, I looked up and saw her walking in front of me. I can still see her with her bright orange blouse, long, blue pleated skirt and bobby socks. She looked gorgeous.

No longer fatigued, I sprung to my feet and quickly asked her if I could take her to dinner at the college diner and afterward to the music program that very night.

"I would love to go with you," she said with music in her voice and a smile on her face.

"I'll pick you up at the girl's dorm at 6," I said.

"I don't live at the dorm; I reside with a faculty family off campus."

"Where is that?" I inquired.

She scribbled a map for me to that house. I had to take a country road up a hill without any street lights. I knew it would be dark by 6, but I was too proud to tell her of my night blindness. Since I wanted to impress her, I didn't ask her to meet me on campus by the auditorium.

Lee was my very first date, so I was anxious about making a good impression. I purchased a half-dozen yellow rose buds arranged in a beautiful corsage. I started up the dark dusty road, not quite sure where I was going. Before I knew it, I had strayed into a plowed-up field. I prayed, "Oh Lord, may there be no bridges or creeks in my way." I saw house lights in the distance, so I decided to go there and ask for directions to the house. I was relieved to discover that it was the right house. She was all ready, dressed in a long, beautiful formal blue dress. The yellow rose corsage went well with her attire. On our way back to the campus, I asked Lee if she would hold my hand.

"Hold your hand?" she retorted with some indignation in her voice. "This is a Christian college with strict rules about dating. This is only our first date, and I am a Christian girl."

"Yes, I understand all that, and I don't mean any offense, but I can't see at night," I humbly replied.

She refused to believe me until I stumbled into a ditch by the side of the road. She guided me back to the campus by allowing me to hold on to her left elbow. I was embarrassed. I thought our relationship would end before it began. What woman would want to lead a man around the rest of her life? I have learned never to underestimate Lee's compassion and dedication to God. The most important advantage going for me was Lee's desire to find a man who had the blessing of God on his life.

It was good that I asked her for the date when I did, because another student had her on his mind. On the Monday following our Friday date, he approached me. "I saw her first," he said, gritting his teeth. "She is in my Greek class. I planned to ask her to go out with me last Friday, but an emergency happened back home, so I had to leave for the weekend. Back off! I am serious about her. Besides, she is a sensitive soul, someone you could not appreciate."

He glowered at me, trying to intimidate me by clenching his fist and waving it in my face. I didn't care what he said or did.

Going Steady, Getting Serious

I decided to ask Lee right away to go steady with me. Going steady at Houghton meant guaranteed dates every Friday night for the semester.

She replied, "Going steady means more to me than going steady. It means being engaged to be engaged."

"Well," I replied, "I have to pray about that."

So later in my room, I got down on my knees before God to ask for His counsel. In the past when I prayed about dating a girl there was always a hesitation in my heart, but this time a perfect peace came over me, so I told Lee, "Yes, it's OK with God. I can go steady with you."

"Wait a minute," she said. "You misunderstood me. I am not ready for that kind of commitment." But we started dating anyway.

One morning Lee and I unintentionally met in the classroom building. She was on her way to her Botany class and I was going to my Latin class. I said good morning to her. The Dean of Men was behind us. "I caught you!" he said. "Come to my office this afternoon." I found out that he was reviving an outdated fifty-year-old rule that prohibited a boy and his girlfriend from meeting before 8 a.m. The Dean of Men campused us for a week, which meant no date or communication of any kind could take place between us for seven days. That seemed like an eternity to me.

We were upset at the unfairness of it, but he made an exception and allowed us to go on a gospel team together along with a chaperone. Lee accompanied me to a church where she gave her testimony and I preached. On our way back to school, she cuddled close to me and whispered softly in my ear so no one else in the car could hear, "Yes!"

I asked her what she meant.

"Yes—I will go steady with you." We sealed our commitment with a kiss, a sweet kiss that I will never forget. Fortunately, our chaperone was sitting in the front seat with the driver and did not see us. If she had reported us, we would have been campused for a month!

Most of the school year was happy for us, but there were a few difficulties to face. We were in love, but not everyone appreciated it. The wife of a faculty member thought we made a bad match. She warned Lee, "You know, if you marry him, your children will look Jewish."

"That's great!" she replied. "Jewish children are beautiful." That woman did not know that Lee's mother's maiden name was Hyman, which is a Hebrew name meaning "to live."

We had a number of interesting episodes during our courtship. Lee is an "outdoors person." One beautiful day, she suggested, "Let's find a comfortable location in the countryside where we can study together for our final exams." We blissfully went through the woods and under a single wire to a clearing between a few trees. We put down a blanket, opened our books and began to study. After a few minutes, Lee jumped to her feet and asked me nervously, "Does a bull have a ring in its nose?"

"Yes, why are you asking?"

"Look!" she shouted, pointing to a bull staring at us from behind a tree. The bull began digging his right front hoof into the ground and kicking the dirt over his shoulder. It looked to me like he was getting ready to charge us.

"What are we going to do?" Lee shouted at me.

"Can you climb a tree?" I replied.

"Yes!"

"Start climbing that tree!" I ordered.

Two feet up, Lee stopped, looked down at me, and asked, "What are you going to do?"

"I am climbing the tree right behind you—keep going!"

When we were safely out of the reach of the bull, I shouted at him, "In the name of the Lord Jesus, go back to your barn." The bull looked startled but unconcerned. He bellowed and from behind the trees a few timid cows appeared. Sniffing at our blankets and books they all finally sauntered away. Unknowingly we had settled down in the cows' path. The bull was simply protecting the herd. When it appeared safe, we climbed down from the tree, grabbed our things and escaped under the wire. From that day on, we did our studying at the library. The angel of the Lord had been watching over us once again.

During the Christmas holidays, I went with Lee to meet her parents. They had no idea how serious we were. We kept that as our secret. One very cold night, Lee's mother asked me to help her hang up Christmas lights. While we were working together outside, I made the mistake of calling her "Mom." She frowned and snapped, "Don't rush things, young man." She went inside the house, slamming the door behind her, leaving me out in the cold.

Lee came to Brooklyn on the train from upstate New York to meet my mother and sisters. I was not too happy about it because of my anxiety over her possible negative reaction to my family. I underestimated Lee's gracious spirit. My biggest problem was telling Lee that my mother wasn't a Christian. My mother wanted to make a good impression on the Christian girl I was bringing home, so she greeted her with, "Praise the Lord!" My mother had learned to "talk the talk" at the mission years before. Later, my mother took me aside and asked me, "So how am I doing?" I unsuccessfully pleaded with her to tell Lee how she really felt about Christianity. I realize now that my mother wanted acceptance.

My mother took to Lee right away. She told me, "Don't let such a wonderful girl get away." My sister Florence appreciated Lee so much that she gave me $150 to buy an engagement ring.

Meeting my mother almost ended my relationship with Lee. She wondered why I would lie about my mother. Lee didn't want a liar for a husband. All the way back to school on the bus, she was planning how to break up with me. Back at Houghton College, she told me what was on her mind. I was devastated. I prayed hard for God to intervene on my behalf. A few hours later she called to say that she was not going to break up with me because God showed her that it was the devil that was trying to break us up. "I am not going to let him do it," she said.

It was six months after my first date with Lee, during the spring break, that I planned to ask Lee to marry me. Just before I did, I knelt down in prayer, thanking God for giving me such a wonderful sweetheart. I requested that God would always enable me to support Lee and our future children. I feared failing my family. Throughout the years, the Lord has kept on answering that prayer in miraculous ways.

After my commencement, Lee went home to prepare for the wedding on August 8, 1953. I stayed at summer school to complete my academic studies at Houghton College. Every Friday afternoon, I hitchhiked 250 miles to see Lee for the weekend.

A few days before the ceremony Lee asked me, "How much money do we have?"

I told her, "After paying off all my school debts, I am broke. Can you loan me $2 for the wedding license?" Without a word of complaint or worry, she joyously gave it to me.

I explained how I had been living by faith for many years and had never missed my three meals a day. We agreed to plan our honeymoon by faith, as if we already had the money. We made our reservations at Happy Acres, a resort in Connecticut. We told only God of our financial predicament. Unbeknownst to us, Lee's mother had told her friends that she wasn't sure of our plans, so a gift of money would be appreciated. At our wedding reception, people handed us gifts of money enough for a wonderful honeymoon.

On to Seminary

We returned from our honeymoon to spend the rest of the summer at Lee's parents' home. A letter of acceptance from the Eastern Baptist Theological Seminary was waiting for us when we got back. Up until that time I had never expected to go on to graduate school.

I regretted that we did not have enough money for Lee to finish college as we had planned. Without a complaint, Lee took a job with a telephone company to help me finish my education. God had given me an amazingly unselfish woman.

I studied under interesting and challenging professors. My professor of cultural anthropology had earned two doctorate degrees, one in medicine and the other in anthropology. He had emigrated from the Republic of Georgia in the former Soviet Union. During the first class, he came over to me, positioned himself less than five inches away from my nose, looked at me straight in the face and demanded with his thick accent: "What's your name, Bolshevik?"

I thought he was joking. His accent hit my funny bone; I lost all self-control. I laughed so hard tears filled my eyes. I just could not answer him.

I was in trouble, so I decided to go to his office and apologize. In the course of our chat, I told him that I was Jewish. His angry frown turned to a delightful smile. "Oh, I love the Jews; God blesses those who love the Jews." Before I left, he gave me a bear hug. All was forgiven. We became the best of friends and before I finished the semester I had acquired an appreciation and understanding of cultural differences.

I spent a profitable year at the seminary, but after nine long years of schooling completing high school, Bible college, getting my degree at Houghton College and taking a year at seminary, I was tired of school and eager to get into ministry. My wife was also ready to settle down and start a family.

Going into a ministry was my greatest desire, but my poor eyesight was a hindrance. On several occasions, I tried to get a driver's license but failed the eye test. The last day at seminary, I decided to try again to get a license.

I prayed, "Lord, You know that last summer I failed my eye test for a driver's license. Up until now, I have had adequate vision to study, but now I need to drive a car in order to serve You better. My wife can't chauffeur me around the rest of my life. By faith, I am going to take an eye examination today. Please grant me the vision required to obtain a license."

At the vehicle department, I nervously waited for my turn to read the eye chart. To my amazement I passed the eye examination easily—and have done so ever since in a number of states and Canada. God continues to give me vision good enough to read, to work on my computer and to drive a car. The Lord never denied me anything I needed to fulfill His will for my life.

CHAPTER SEVEN

Learning on the Job

I will instruct you and teach you in the way you
should go;
I will counsel you and watch over you.
(Psalm 32:8)

Learning to Be a Pastor

I left seminary to accept a call to be the pastor of the Union Church in southern New Jersey. The church was located in a resort town with about 200 year-round citizens and thousands of tourists in the summer. The town fathers established the church to serve all the people of the community, regardless of their beliefs. No doctrinal adherence was required for membership. The main event of the church year was putting on a rummage sale and barbecue to raise money for the church budget. The church was the center of the local political structure and everyone who was anybody in town unofficially belonged to the church.

I joyously accepted the call to the church because it was my first opportunity to become a pastor. Had I been wiser, I would have sought a position as an assistant pastor to be mentored by an experienced leader. I was too proud at the time to work under anyone. I presumed my academic education was enough training for me to take over the leadership of a church. I couldn't have been more wrong! Every morning I woke up not knowing what to do with my time.

A formal education provides the opportunity of developing many necessary skills for the ministry. In school one can acquire the skill of interpreting Scripture from the original languages, the ability to theologize by applying biblical principles to current issues, the understanding of contemporary cultures and the acquisition of communication skills in speaking and writing. However, I lacked the practical experience that can mature those skills.

In truth, I learned more from my failures than from my successes. My inadequacies became apparent during my first funeral. An elderly lady had died. Since I did not know the deceased and no one wanted to talk about her, I gave no eulogy. After the service, someone told me, "We were just waiting for you to say how wonderful she was in her lifetime. If you had, we would have burst out laughing. The woman was the town drunk."

At the burial site, a comedy of errors took place. Enormous, bloodthirsty mosquitoes filled the air, attacking us mercilessly again and again. I wanted to escape into the safety of my car before I needed a blood transfusion. Unfortunately, I had to wait until the ceremony was over. The pallbearers gently placed her casket on a scaffold over an open grave; then without warning the casket fell through the framework six feet down into the grave. We all heard her body hit the side of the casket with a thump. We stood there in hushed shock. Her daughter, standing at the foot of the grave, fainted and fell into it, landing on top of her mother's casket. It took her two muscular brothers to lift her out.

I wondered how this could be happening to me at my first funeral. The worst part of the scenario was my inability to stop laughing out loud because of nervousness. Everyone else looked aghast at me. I had completely humiliated myself. What a way to start my ministry in a small town where everyone knows everybody's business. I had a lot to learn!

I was about to learn about conflicts in a church as well. Until I went to the Union Church, I had an unrealistic view of the ministry. I expected to find only unity and peace but found that Christians can disagree strongly. Just before I arrived at the church, a struggle for the leadership of the church had taken place. My many years of theological education did not prepare me to deal diplomatically with internal conflict.

At a board meeting, a leading layman proposed using the money raised specifically for a new parsonage to pay off the old mortgage on the Christian education wing. Then at a future time, they would obtain a full mortgage for the parsonage. His intention was honorable. He just wanted to save some interest on their present loan. Out of my inexperience, I opposed his recommendation. I was concerned about a possible negative reaction from the congregation. I explained, "The congregation expects the parsonage to get underway immediately." I wanted to protect the board's credibility with the donors. My intention was not to incriminate anyone, but I unwisely said, "We don't want to look as if we are misappropriating funds." I should not have used the word "misappropriating"; the elder thought that I was attacking his integrity. Certainly that was not in my thinking. The board agreed with my perspective on the issue at the time. I won my point but lost the support of the elder.

Months later, at the dedication of the new parsonage, he took me aside and said, "I am going to destroy you!" The intensity of his emotions frightened me. I tried hard to reassure him that I had no intention of accusing him of any impropriety. I even apologized for opposing his motion. On the surface everything quieted down. He acted very pleasant with me so I assumed all was forgiven and forgotten. I could not have been more wrong.

The night before the annual congregational meeting, a member came to see me. "Pastor, I think you should know what the elder and his allies are plotting. Tomorrow night they will make a motion to fire you. Their secret plan is all set up to take the congregation by surprise. They have persuaded a number of our summer members to come and support their effort. I was promised that if I voted against you, he would make me an elder of the church. Pastor, everyone knows I am unworthy of eldership. I cannot go along with them. I wanted you to be aware of the situation."

There wasn't enough time to inform the entire congregation of the plot to dismiss me, and the summer people did not know me well enough to support me. My only option was to pray. I got down on my knees and opened the Bible for a word from God. Psalm 50:15 was the first passage I read: "Call upon me in the day of trouble; I will deliver you, and you will honor me."

I prayed, "Oh Lord, if I fail so quickly in my first assignment, I will never be sure You ever called me to serve You. We have no money reserves. How will I support my wife and our unborn child? They rely on me. How can I face my fellow seminary students? I would be ashamed to fail You. Lord, please deliver me and I will glorify You. In the name of Your Son, Jesus, I pray. Amen."

While I was tossing and turning in a troubled sleep, God was at work. An unexpected blizzard hit the entire area from the New Jersey coast to Philadelphia. All the roads were closed to traffic. The congregational meeting was postponed for a month, which gave enough time for the secret plot to leak out to the entire congregation. Their scheme fell apart.

Later, a few of my opponents told me, "We had the votes to get rid of you, but we perceived the hand of God was in the storm. We will try our best to work with you." God had answered my prayer and preserved my call to ministry.

I told my friend Dr. Lehman Strauss about my unpleasant episode. "Al," he groaned, "wherever you go in the future, you will always find conflict waiting for you." I didn't want to hear that bad news, but the good news was that Jesus would also be there to sustain me. Scripture verses like Psalm 34:4-5, 7 describe my life very well: "I sought the LORD, and he answered me; he delivered me from all my fears. Those who look to him are radiant; their faces are never covered with shame. . . . The angel of the LORD encamps around those who fear him, and he delivers them."

Since I believed in missions, I appointed a study committee to develop a missionary strategy for the church. After six months of studying the issue, the chairperson made her report to the congregation: "After much evaluation by our committee, we have concluded that charity begins at home. We can't afford to give away any money to missions." I could not believe my ears. I felt it was time to resign my position and go on to my next assignment from God.

Learning to Be a Missionary

After two years at the church, I felt an obligation to witness to my own Jewish people under the American Board of Missions to the Jews, which is now known as the Chosen People's Ministry. Dr. Leopold Cohn, who had been a rabbi for many years in Austria, founded the mission. One day as he was reading the 9th chapter from the prophet Daniel, he came across verses 25 and 26:

> Know and understand this: From the issuing of the decree to restore and rebuild Jerusalem until the Anointed One, the ruler, comes, there will be seven "sevens," and sixty-two "sevens." It will be rebuilt with streets and a trench, but in times of trouble. After the sixty-two "sevens," the Anointed One will be cut off and will have nothing. The people of the ruler who will come will destroy the city and the sanctuary. The end will come like a flood: War will continue until the end, and desolations have been decreed.

Rabbi Cohn realized that this prophecy predicted that the Messiah would come and die before the destruction of the second Temple. In his search to find the identity of the Messiah, he found Jesus, the true Messiah. Out of his love for Israel, he began the first mission to the Jews in the United States. As a child, I first heard that Jesus was the Messiah at their Brooklyn branch. It was there that I had first experienced the true love of God.

My becoming a Jewish missionary in New York City horrified and embarrassed my beloved mother. She tried to keep my new career a secret from our relatives by telling them I was a high school teacher. My aunts and uncles loved bragging about their successful adult children—"My daughter, the doctor," "My son, the lawyer" or "My boy, the businessman." How could my Jewish mother boast, "My son, the missionary"? She couldn't keep her secret for long. One of my cousins saw me preaching on the street and told everyone in the family that I had become an apostate.

As a young missionary, I was trained under the old-fashioned concepts of hard work, long hours and accountability to the person in authority over me. The mission leaders did not believe they owed me a living because I was an ordained minister, a Jewish Christian and a good person; they expected me to be productive. The policy of the mission was to start a new worker at the bottom. Even though I had been a pastor, I was assigned to assist a woman missionary. Miss Hilda Koser was a hard-working missionary who was successful in winning Jewish people to Jesus because she loved them. She led a congregation of over 100 Jewish believers. She was like a protective mother hen over her chicks.

Right from the beginning of our association, I knew she was the boss. Being a child of the Mission was my one redeeming factor in her eyes. She told me, "My first consideration is the people under my care. If you don't serve them well, you will have to leave." I soon learned from her example that the object of the ministry was not for personal fulfillment, but for the benefit of God's people.

I gave weekly reports of my activities and results to Miss Koser. Although there were times I thought she was an unreasonable taskmaster, I thank God she wasn't easy on me, because she taught me how to work effectively. Miss Koser shaped me into a mentor of other young pastors and missionaries.

After a year, Miss Koser paid me the greatest compliment possible. For the first time in her ministry, she took a vacation to Hawaii and left me in complete charge of her ministry. Never before had she ever trusted anyone else with her precious flock.

Lee and I were then transferred to Lakewood, New Jersey to start a mission branch. Our son David was born there. I drove my wife twenty miles through a blizzard to get her to the hospital on time. The state police warned people to stay off the road. All along the road there were abandoned cars in ditches.

Finally we arrived. I waited for hours for the delivery, walking the floor in the father's waiting room. A nurse told me that I should go home, as it would be a long time before the baby came. Slowly and carefully, I drove back home through the blizzard. I went to bed and quickly fell into a deep asleep. I was awakened by a phone call from the hospital. Lee happily announced that we had a beautiful son. She insisted that I drive right back to the hospital to see my baby boy. Off I went back into the blizzard. I did not want to disappoint my wife.

My missionary efforts were not very successful in Lakewood, so I was transferred again to represent the mission to churches in upstate New York. My purpose was to open up churches for our mission to the Jews. I discovered sincere interest and a genuine love for the Jewish people among the pastors of evangelical churches.

I pointed out to the churches that right after Pentecost, the Jewish disciples neglected the evangelization of the Gentiles. They only preached the gospel to fellow Jews. Those early followers of Jesus believed that salvation belonged only to their nation, not to the world. God had to deal with the prejudice of Simon Peter against Gentiles. It took the repetition of a vision three times and the audible command of the Lord to persuade Peter to go into the house of Cornelius, to a Roman centurion, an uncircumcised Gentile to preach the gospel. (See Acts 10:9-23.) Peter and his Jewish colleagues were amazed to witness Gentiles being baptized with the Spirit as they were on Pentecost.

Acts 10:34-35 reveals the change of Peter's attitude toward Gentiles. "Then Peter began to speak: 'I now realize how true it is that God does not show favoritism but accepts men from every nation who fear him and do what is right.' "

Since the church is now predominately Gentile, the situation has reversed itself. There are some theologians who assert that God is now finished with the Jews. They express no interest in sharing the gospel with them. They claim that all the blessings of Israel belong to the Church, while all the woes, judgments and curses still belong to Israel. They do not rightly interpret the Scriptures. I believe the reason that the Word of God declares that salvation is to the Jew first is to remind Gentile Christians of their obligation not to forget Israel in their evangelistic efforts. God has made Jewish evangelism a top priority of the Church. A good number of churches responded well to my exhortation.

On one preaching trip, I was nearly killed. It happened when I was about thirty years old. I was driving home from Buffalo on the New York State Thruway after preaching at a prophecy conference. I was anxious to see my family, so I wasn't paying much attention to my speed. A car approaching me from the opposite lane kept blinking his headlights on and off, which I interpreted to mean there were police and radar up ahead. I glanced down at my speedometer and saw that I was driving at seventy-five miles an hour, fifteen miles above the speed limit. I took my foot off of the accelerator, slowing down to less than thirty miles an hour. I am not sure why I reduced my speed so radically.

Just when I was about to speed up again, my left rear tire blew out. I struggled to keep my car under control. I finally pulled over to the shoulder of the road and stopped safely without a scratch. I sat there by the side of the highway for some time, shaking and thanking God for sparing me. A few weeks prior, I had temporarily replaced my rear tire in need of repair with a nearly worn-out spare tire. I had forgotten to put my good tire back on before taking the trip. If my tire had blown out while I was going seventy-five miles an hour, I might not be alive to write my book. My carelessness would have left a young, brokenhearted widow with four young children to raise alone.

After I replaced my tire, I drove on, but I never saw a policeman anywhere on the highway. What possessed that other driver to flick his headlights on and off warning me of danger ahead? The angel of the Lord was on the job. The Bible tells us about angels in the writings of the Jewish prophet, Isaiah: "And the angel of his presence saved them. In his love and mercy he redeemed them" (Isaiah 63:9).

Getting Back on Track

My experience as a field representative was short-lived, because being away from my wife and young children for long periods of time did not seem right to me. Because I wanted to work with people as a pastor and missionary, I applied for a new assignment.

I accepted the directorship of the Pittsburgh mission branch as my new ministry. For four years I developed a messianic congregation. While progress was slow, I witnessed the power of Jesus at work in many Jewish lives, proving His messianic authenticity. I remember the joy of leading a Jewish woman to Christ. Her husband was very upset about her faith in Jesus.

One day she came to see me. She said, "You know my husband is not a Christian. A month ago he told me, 'Your Jesus spoke to me. He asked me, "Are you ready?" I am not ready to die!' I told him, 'You are working too hard. It is just your imagination.' "

A month later he complained of a severe headache and collapsed. He was rushed to the hospital. The diagnosis was not good. He had a large, fast-growing cancerous tumor on his brain. An emergency operation took place, but the prognosis was poor. The surgeon said to the man's wife, "It is unlikely he will ever come out of the coma. I expect he will die shortly."

I prayed, "Oh Lord, before he dies, give him one more chance to know You."

As we entered intensive care, he opened his eyes and sat up. He surprised me by saying, "Oh Pastor Runge, you have the most important job in the world." He knew that he was going to die, and gladly accepted Jesus as his Messiah and Savior. He thanked us for coming; then he said he was tired. He closed his eyes and went to sleep. Edith and I left believing God had healed him, but he died just a few minutes later. We told the surgeon about our last conversation with him. "I don't see how it is possible," he said. "We had to remove too much of his brain trying to save his life."

One of my greatest joys was to lead Les Rubinstein, a young businessman with a bright future, to Christ. He was a logical thinker. He asked two legitimate questions that are on the minds of most Jews. First, he asked how Jesus could be the Messiah when the prophets predicted that when the Messiah comes, he would bring peace and justice to the world. Where then is world peace and justice?

I pointed out that the prophet Isaiah also predicted that the Messiah must first come to suffer and die as our atonement to bring forgiveness and reconciliation to the world. I pointed him to Isaiah 53:4-6:

> Surely he took up our infirmities
> and carried our sorrows,

yet we considered him stricken by God,
smitten by him, and afflicted.
But he was pierced for our transgressions,
he was crushed for our iniquities;
the punishment that brought us peace
was upon him,
and by his wounds we are healed.
We all, like sheep, have gone astray,
each of us has turned to his own way;
and the LORD has laid on him
the iniquity of us all.

Les then asked, "Where does it say in our Jewish Bible that the Messiah is God?"

I pointed out a number of Old Testament verses that referred to the Messiah as Deity, such as Isaiah 9:6: "For to us a child is born, to us a son is given, and the government will be on his shoulders. And he will be called Wonderful Counselor, Mighty God, Everlasting Father, Prince of Peace."

As a Jewish boy growing up in Brooklyn, I was unacquainted with messianic prophecies in the Bible. I had never struggled with the question, "How could a genuinely inspired Jewish prophet like Isaiah call a human child Mighty God and Everlasting Father?" Years went by before I discovered and understood this mystery. The Jewish prophet was predicting the coming of Jesus the Messiah and revealing His true identity.

Long before Les came to see me, he realized that the Judaism of his background was based on the development of man-made traditions. Eventually, he acknowledged Jesus as his Savior and Lord. I had the privilege of performing his wedding to a beautiful and godly woman. Together they have been active as authentic witnesses of God's love.

Some of my biggest disappointments in Jewish missionary work were watching people come close to faith in Jesus but then turn away. After I led a young Jewish man to Christ, his mother began attending our weekly Bible study. She became convinced that Jesus was the Messiah, so I asked her to receive Jesus as her Lord and Savior. She replied, "I am not ready. I want my husband to come to Christ with me." He told her that if she became a Christian, he would divorce her. She not only gave up the conviction she had acquired, but she also opposed her son's faith.

Years later, I met her son, who was on the pastoral staff of an evangelical church. I asked him about his mother. "She's not doing very well," he replied. He then informed me of his family's troubles. Their business had gone bankrupt. His father had divorced his mother to marry a younger woman who had worked at their store. Unknown to her, he had been having an affair for some time. He wanted to use her interest in Jesus as a justification to leave her. The Lord knew all about the troubles that were about to fall on her and He had wanted to be there for her but she had rejected Him.

Learning to Preach on the Radio

The old idea of a long-term ministry in one specific place isn't always God's will for us. Sometimes God assigns us to new ventures in order to increase our skills and prepare us for future opportunities. Such was my situation when I began desiring a radio ministry. Since there wasn't any opportunity to take over the Chosen People's radio ministry, I gladly accepted the gracious invitation of Dr. Charles Halff to share in his Christian Jew Hour radio ministry.

I had always aspired to become an influential and a well-known international Bible teacher. My ambitious desire seemed about to come to pass. Charles gave me that opportunity. I made ten audition tapes. The response from the radio listeners was positive and I was hired. One of the things I appreciated most about Charles was the freedom he gave me to preach in my own style. Hard work was the way he built his ministry, and I learned from him how to create, build and administer a Christian organization.

I had never realized before how many authentic Christians there are in the world. My biggest pleasure was reading the inspiring mail from our listeners. I especially remember a letter from a faithful listener. It went something like this,

> Dear Brothers,
>
> I heard your wonderful broadcast and your need for financial support. I am an elderly widow with limited funds. I just ran out of coal for the potbelly stove which heats my house. I only have $5 left until my Social Security check arrives next week. I am sending my $5 to you for the ministry instead of buying coal. I will be all right. I plan to wear my overcoat in the house until my check arrives.

After reading hundreds of such sacrificial letters, I concluded that genuine Christianity still abounds in our land.

Learning to Tithe

While in San Antonio, Texas, we attended a Southern Baptist Church, where tithing was preached often and without apology. Since we were giving our full time to the ministry, I felt that somehow we were exempt from tithing. Our pastor, Jack Taylor, was one of the most inspiring preachers I had ever heard. One Sunday, he pointed out that even the ancient Jewish priests who were supported by the tithe of Israel were commanded to participate in tithing. I could no longer justify my stinginess with God, so I decided to tithe and trust Him for my financial needs.

Just after I made this decision, the manager of the apartment complex where we were living came to me and ordered me to take my family and move out. It seemed that my little children had rescued baby birds from the trash bin where the men who had been cleaning nests out of the drains had disposed of them. No apology was acceptable; we had to leave.

We wanted to buy a house, but we had no money for a down payment. So I got very specific with the Lord about our need for housing. "Lord, grant to us a house with four bedrooms, with a bath and a half. Please add air-conditioning, a two-car garage and a fenced yard for our children to play in. Remember, Lord, we don't have any money for a down payment."

God provided in an amazing way. A few days later, I was shopping at a drugstore and overheard an Air Force officer tell the pharmacist, "My superior had promised me at least five years in the city, so I built a house for my family. Now I have orders to leave for Europe with my family within a couple of weeks. Do you know anyone who wants to buy a house without a down payment?"

"No," the pharmacist replied.

I shouted across the store, "I do!"

The house was everything that I had asked God for. I could never have gotten a house with no down payment, but the military officer was entitled to that benefit. He was able to pass that on to me. I learned that tithing is an act of trust in the God who is the Giver of all good and perfect gifts.

Learning about My Giftedness

It is important to discover our giftedness because it is God's job description for our lives. For some time, I was experiencing a growing conviction that my giftedness and calling in life was to be a pastor, not a missionary, not a fund-raiser and not a radio Bible teacher. I resisted it, especially since I was experiencing success. How could I give up preaching daily to a potential audience of millions through radio to become a pastor of a small congregation? A powerful struggle was going on inside of me.

Finally the light dawned on me. My ultimate meaning could only be found in the center of God's will. I surrendered my self-serving ambitions to God. I decided that it was better for me to be the pastor of a little country church in the back woods within the will of God than to be an internationally renowned radio Bible preacher outside of it.

CHAPTER EIGHT

A Bumpy Road Ahead

Therefore, my dear brothers, stand firm. Let nothing move you. Always give yourselves fully to the work of the Lord, because you know that your labor in the Lord is not in vain. (1 Corinthians 15:58)

One of the joys in looking back over a ministry is reflecting on God's work in the people of the church under my care. Watching God's transforming grace turn sinners into saints, misers into generous givers, the fearful into visionaries and the mean-spirited into compassionate and gracious people made my every effort and sacrifice worthwhile. Not everyone responded well to my ministry, but a number of the most troublesome people later became my good friends and supporters. Remembering the early struggles with God's good-intentioned people brings back a few tears but a lot more joy. Sharing episodes of my struggles with difficulties is in no way meant to embarrass anyone, for these are the common experiences of most congregations.

Lee and I had made the decision that whatever the personal cost might be for us, we would allow the Lord to decide on our placement in His vineyard. We promised the Lord that we would accept the first church that gave me a unanimous call, no questions asked. I determined never again to allow my ministry to be determined by the potential of the opportunity to enhance my reputation or by the size of my salary.

I sent out résumés to all the District Superintendents of The Christian and Missionary Alliance, informing them of my availability. Rev. Richard Bailey of the New England District was the first one to reply by phone. He was acquainted with my ministry because I had preached a series of prophetic messages for him at a summer Bible conference. "Al," Rev. Bailey said, "I believe you are the right man for the North Avenue Alliance Church in Burlington, Vermont."

Lee and I weren't even sure where the state of Vermont was located. The map indicated it was in cold country. The church board felt it could not afford to fly both my wife and me to candidate. So I went alone. Lee trusted me to make the right decision. Since my experience with flying was limited at the time, I had a phobia of flying. After kissing my wife good-bye at the airport, I boarded the plane with some trepidation. I buckled up in my seat.

On the flight, the plane was bounced around by a terrible storm. The pilot announced we were unable to land at our destination. I prayed harder than I ever had before. I feared we were all going to die, and my heart was pounding. How humiliating it would have been for me to die of a heart attack over an accident that never happened! But God speaks to me with insights of wisdom. The Lord reminded me that my lifetime had already been determined and was in His hands. I could go through life with a positive or a negative attitude. I could worry or I could trust the Lord: the choice was mine. I decided to trust the Lord and relax. I opened my Bible at random to find some consolation and I read: "Your love, O LORD, reaches to the heavens, your faithfulness to the skies" (Psalm 36:5).

It was God's personal word for me that His faithfulness follows me wherever I go. All my fear evaporated, and I had a most enjoyable flight.

In less than five hours, I flew northeast from warm and sunny San Antonio into a Vermont snowstorm. As the plane descended below the clouds to land at the airport, I beheld a most beautiful sight. The scene below me was a picturesque, snow-covered Vermont town with puffs of smoke ascending from the chimneys of tiny houses.

A board member met me at the airport and drove me through a blinding snowstorm. The windshield wipers of his car weren't working. We kept stopping to wipe the snow and ice off the windshield. I began wondering if we were going to make it, but God got us safely to the motel. On Sunday morning, I preached to less than a hundred people, sharing my life story with the congregation.

I delight in being Jewish, and I don't care who knows it. I had heard rumors that a well-known Bible teacher was also a Hebrew Christian, so when I met him at a Bible conference one time, I introduced myself as a fellow Jew. He took me aside and whispered to me, "Don't ever tell anyone you are a Jew. In the ministry, it will work against you." He tried to hide his identity but to no avail; everyone suspected he was Jewish. I have always been honest about my ethnic background, and I don't want any opportunity that is based on deception. My decision to be candid has only enhanced my opportunities. On all four occasions when I was interviewed for a pastor's position, I was called. I even received calls from churches where I didn't candidate. I have found that the overwhelming majority of evangelicals love the Jews. They are the best friends of the nation of Israel.

The Vermont board interviewed me that very Sunday evening after I preached. I told the Lord if I received a unanimous call that night before I flew home, I would view it as a sign from Him and accept the call with no questions asked.

The proper proscribed procedure would have been for the board first to inform the District Superintendent of their decision, and he then would notify me. After the interview, the board bypassed the policy and invited me to be their pastor. I took this as an indication of God's leading.

The chairman wanted to discuss my salary before I left town, but I refused to talk about money. I said, "I trust you businessmen to be fair with me. You know what it takes to support a family with four children in Burlington."

I never wanted to make my ministry a matter of dollars and cents. My answer made them very happy. (Later I came to realize the importance of negotiating for my wage!) I did not tell the board what I was making at the time. After I arrived with my family, I found out that I would be paid one-third of what I was making as a radio Bible teacher. We moved into a small parsonage with two bedrooms, one bath and an attic, where my two sons were to sleep.

The leaders promised me that if their church prospered financially under my ministry, so would I. Their word was good enough for me. I returned home with the good and bad news. I told my wife of our call and informed her that we would have to sacrifice at first, but the board would eventually raise our standard of living. My wife kept the budget in balance. As I look back on those days, I don't know how she did it. The only time we borrowed money on our credit card was to give our children a decent Christmas. It usually took us an entire year to pay the debt off.

After we arrived in Vermont, I discovered the state was considered to be the graveyard of evangelicalism. Less than one-half of one percent of the county had any evangelical background. I wondered what I had gotten myself into. A few weeks after we moved to Burlington, a young Jewish man whom I had led to Christ in Pittsburgh called me. He was the acting chairman of the board of his church, a large congregation of over 800 members where I had preached for a week of revival meetings. He informed me that his church was giving me a call to become its pastor. What a powerful moment of temptation for me! After a brief struggle within myself, I decided that it would be unethical to break my commitment to the Vermont church. I thanked Les and asked him to convey my deepest regrets to the board. I wished that he had called me a month before!

Financial Difficulties

From the very beginning of my ministry, the Lord blessed the Vermont church with increased attendance and financial income. Since the church's income nearly tripled that year, we anticipated a raise of at least $5 a week, just what we needed to buy our children new clothes for school. The board met without me to review my wage. The next day, I waited for the call that did not come. I decided to call the treasurer myself to find out what they had decided. Stammering nervously, he said, "The board decided not to give you a raise this year."

I was stunned. "Why?" I inquired. "Are you satisfied with my ministry?"

"Yes, of course we are!" he assured me. He suggested that I speak to the elder who had vigorously opposed my raise. Every church board seems to have at least one member who objects to wage raises for the pastor. Such a person does not practice the golden rule of Jesus, "Do unto others as you would have them do to you." Perhaps it is because he thinks that a truly spiritual pastor isn't concerned about material things.

I went to the objector's office for a chat. I asked the elder point-blank if he was satisfied with my ministry.

"Absolutely!" he declared emphatically with an approving smile. "Pastor, you are doing a marvelous job."

"So why didn't you give me a raise?"

He huffed and puffed. "Just because we have money in the bank doesn't mean we should give it away."

I sensed his uneasiness, so I allowed him to change the subject. Later in the conversation, he began complaining about his own financial situation.

"Listen, my boss promised me a $15,000 Christmas bonus, but only gave me $10,000."

I couldn't believe my ears. How could he compare his financial situation with mine? All I expected was a meager $5 a week more. Somehow I could not find any sympathy in my heart for my friend.

I finally got my $5 raise because I shamed the board into giving it to me. I will never forget another man who voted against everything that cost money. Since he was one of the wealthiest and most influential members in the church, he intimidated me. One day the treasurer said, "Maybe I shouldn't tell you this, but you should know that that man who has so much to say against your recommendations hasn't given a dime to this church."

Later I discovered his attitude about giving stemmed from a childhood experience. He told me that when he was eleven years old, he had worked and saved his money to purchase a shortwave radio. Without his knowledge and consent, his father gave it away to a missionary who needed one.

Although it had taken place forty years ago, he still spoke about it with deep emotion. True, his father had no right to give away what belonged to him, but that wasn't an excuse to be stingy with God's work. I changed his mind about opposing church projects by reminding him that the money needed did not come out of his own pocket. I saw the light of understanding come to his eyes. From then on he voted for every project I recommended.

God did a very special work in the hearts of the men on the board and within the congregation. Within a short time, the church became the most generous in the New England District of the Alliance. My wage became the highest in the district.

Looking Out for Others

As a member of the Ordination Council of the New England District of the Alliance while in Vermont, I developed a deep concern for the underpaid pastors of our district. Many of them lived below the poverty line. Some depended on government food stamps to get by. In my Jewish upbringing, I was taught to care about people less fortunate than I. The New Testament also reiterates interest in the material needs of God's servants. The Bible tells us in First Corinthians 9:9-11:

> For it is written in the Law of Moses: "Do not muzzle an ox while it is treading out the grain." Is it about oxen that God is concerned? Surely he says this for us, doesn't he? Yes, this was written for us, because when the plowman plows and the thresher threshes, they ought to do so in the hope of sharing in the harvest. If we have sown spiritual seed among you, is it too much if we reap a material harvest from you?

At a district conference, I stood up and made a motion that a suggested minimum wage for pastors be instituted for our churches. An elderly man stood up and declared that the day the Alliance sets up a minimum wage for pastors is the day he would leave the Alliance. Another person claimed that there were churches that could not afford to pay their pastors a livable wage. I responded, "If a church can't afford to pay their pastor a livable wage, they will at least understand the sacrifice he is making for them." My motion was turned down two successive years.

The third year I made my motion again. John Carlson, who was one of the patriarchs of the district, spoke up for the motion. He said, "Last year I was elected to our national salary committee. I am not going to tell you what our leaders and missionaries are paid, but this much I will tell you—everyone is well cared for except for our pastors."

The District Conference appointed a committee of businessmen to evaluate the financial needs of a pastor's family. The next year, the committee gave its report. The majority of the delegates accepted their recommendations, and the action was communicated to the district churches. Within a year every congregation met the guidelines, and some did even more for their pastors. Not one church suffered financially by increasing the wages of their pastors—in fact, many prospered. The outcome verified my belief that when a congregation adequately cares for God's servants, He will provide the necessary resources.

An Emotional Roller Coaster

I wasn't prepared for the emotional ups and downs of the pastorate. In one day I could be called on in the morning to comfort a young couple because their baby had been stillborn, and in the afternoon I was expected to celebrate at a wedding.

I spent many sleepless nights over the sorrows of God's people whom I came to love as my own family. I will always remember a Christian couple's concern for their two grown sons. The boys were brought up in the church, but they turned away from the Lord. Late one night they returned home, drunk and disagreeable. Their argument turned nasty. The younger brother got his father's shotgun down and threatened his brother. The parents were awakened by a loud gunshot. They rushed into the living room and saw their younger son in despair stooping down over his wounded and unconscious brother. He was begging for forgiveness and pleading for his brother to wake up. The parents phoned me in the middle of the night and woke me out of a sound sleep. I quickly got dressed and rushed to the hospital. I sat with the distressed parents the entire night trying to comfort them while their critically injured son was in surgery.

"I didn't mean it! I love my brother! He's my best friend," the other son sobbed.

A police officer was waiting with the family. If the brother lived, the charge would be assault with a deadly weapon, but if he died, it would be murder. The grim-faced surgeon came into the waiting room, shaking his head and sadly reporting, "We did all we could to save his life, but we lost him." I witnessed the helplessness of his parents as they watched the officer arrest and handcuff their only surviving son and take him away to prison. The young man was sentenced to forty years in the state penitentiary. A few months later, while in prison, he accepted Christ and found peace with God.

Observing God's Power

Looking back over the years I can clearly see that the ministry has done more for me than I did for it. I was compelled by circumstances to trust God for the impossible. The challenges of ministry, which confronted me daily, caused me to grow in faith.

There were some lessons that I had to learn more than once, especially in the area of healing. In spite of the fact that God healed me of asthma and improved my eyesight, I went through a period of skepticism about the healing ministry available to the church. I should have known better, especially since I had personally experienced His healing touch.

I was forced to deal with the healing ministry when a young woman asked me to arrange for the elders to anoint her. A specialist had examined her eyes and informed her that she was going blind because an inoperable tumor was growing and pressing on her optic nerve. I was hesitant about anointing her with oil, but she insisted. One of the elders, a physician, felt he should excuse himself from the anointing, but at the last minute he reconsidered. We anointed her with oil and prayed for her failing vision. I can't call it a prayer of great faith; nevertheless, God was merciful and healed her completely. Later, Ruth told me that as she was leaving the church her vision was completely restored. Thirty years have gone by and she still sees normally.

I started on the right road of faith in praying for the sick, but as time went by I found myself on a detour of presumption. I assumed that since God still heals the sick, He would heal everyone who sincerely asked for it by faith. A Jewish man came to Christ under my ministry. We became the best of friends. As Jewish Christians we had much in common and thought alike. We especially enjoyed discussing and debating intellectual ideas. Jay took an early retirement from the FBI and filled his days with all sorts of interesting hobbies. He fascinated me by identifying flowers and trees by their Latin names. Coming from the big city of Brooklyn, I knew less than nothing about plants. (My wife had once, and only once, asked me to weed her garden. In ignorance, I plucked up some of her best flowering plants. That was the last time I was invited to help in her garden.)

Jay loved to hear about the Lord Jesus. Spiritually he was growing by leaps and bounds. I was looking forward to a long-term friendship. But one day he started complaining about having serious headaches. A medical examination revealed a brain tumor. I suggested anointing by the elders of the church, assuring him of God's power and willingness to heal. I thought that this was the perfect opportunity given by the Lord Jesus to demonstrate His reality to Jay's Jewish wife. So we anointed and prayed for him in faith, but his headaches increased and the tumor kept on growing. My best friend was dying and I couldn't understand why God was ignoring my personal grief. The surgeons had removed a lot of brain tissue to excise the tumor, but to no avail.

After months of anguish for all of us, I knew Jesus was not going to heal him, and that the time of his death was near. I sat by his bedside in the hospital room. Looking down on my friend in a coma, I observed that his breathing was irregular and laborious. I said, "Jay, Jesus isn't going to heal you. You have fought a good fight of faith. You can now go on to be with Jesus in heaven." Jay's body relaxed, his breathing slowed down and within seconds he died. I could not fully accept it. The Lord had healed others—why not Jay? With his brilliant intellect and zeal for the Lord, Jay would have been an effective witness for Jesus.

I was embarrassed because I had predicted his healing. I knew his wife was watching to see if Jesus could heal her husband. I took Jay's death as a personal failure. While I refused to blame the Lord or get angry with Him, I felt He had let me down. Perplexed, I silently withdrew from praying for the sick. The ministry of healing was too unpredictable for me. I was confused and wondered why God hadn't backed up the promise of healing that I had given in His name. My pride was hurt when my friend died. I felt that God had left me standing there with egg on my face.

Another factor in my hesitancy to pray for the sick was the false claims of healing made by some faith healers. I was asked by a physician to visit an accident victim in a nursing home. At the age of twenty-one, she had been totally paralyzed from her neck down because of an automobile accident. Her doctors told her that she needed an immediate operation to enable her to sit up and have some mobility in a wheelchair. If she wasn't operated on soon, she would be bedridden for life. Two young men anointed her with oil and then prophesied that she would be healed within thirty days. They warned her that if she accepted the operation, God would not heal her.

Thirty days later, she still could not move. The men explained it was only a test of her faith. They prophesied that within another thirty days she would be standing and walking without any assistance. The time came and went, but she was still flat on her back, unable to move. They blamed her lack of faith. By the time she was willing to agree to the operation, it was too late to help her. As far as I know, she is still in that same nursing home with no hope of recovery. Such fanatical behavior increased my reluctance to pray for the sick.

Over the years, I grew hot and cold about the healing ministry of the church. It took me many more years to fully appreciate and understand that healing is subject to God's will—not mine. We human beings are very egocentric. I had to learn that the Lord Jesus is not my servant, obligated to do my bidding, but that I am His servant.

There is a vast difference between faith and presumption. Our Lord expressed true faith in the Garden of Gethsemane, in Matthew 26:39. I believe Jesus was saying, "If there is any other possible way to save mankind than by my suffering and death, let me be spared." He prayed, "My Father, if it be possible, let this cup pass from me: nevertheless not as I will, but as thou wilt" (KJV).

Faith submits to the will of God even if it leads us through suffering and an early death. On the other hand, presumption demands its own way with God. Presumption says to God, "You must do it my way and satisfy my will." Faith says, "Not my will but Thine be done." God's grace, patience and long-suffering truly amaze me. My heavenly Father had every justification to disqualify me from His ministry because of my presumption; instead, He kept patiently working with me.

Always Relevant

Soon after I arrived in Vermont, I had breakfast with a local pastor who had rejected the traditional church. He was the pastor of a congregation of 150 people who owned seven acres of land with an adequate building. Claiming the traditional church was finished, my friend developed a new strategy for the future church. He held a worship service only once a month; he called it "Festival Sunday." He labeled that Sunday as the "church in residence." During the rest of the month, he sent various committees of his members out to be involved in social and political activities. He called those activities the "church in the world." Various sources, including a well-known evangelical professor, called his concept of the church the wave of the future.

I said to my friend, "We hold very different opinions about the future of the church. Only time will test our diverse beliefs. We are developing an evangelical congregation, while you are going in a different direction. I wonder what will become of our churches ten years from now."

More than thirty years have passed since our breakfast together; the North Avenue Alliance Church is now situated on where his seven acres used to be, with a facility that accommodates 700 worshipers.

Making Family My Priority

One of my early mistakes in Vermont was investing most of my emotional and spiritual energies in the church family, leaving little left over for my small children. Fortunately for our children, my wife was supportive of my ministry. Right from the time of her conversion, Lee wanted to be a part of the Lord's work. Her positive attitude about my involvement in the church kept my children from growing resentful over the time I spent away from them. I remember one day my ten-year-old son, David, wanted me to go fishing with him down at the Winooski River. I explained that I wished I could go with him, but I was too busy.

He smiled and said, "I understand, Dad," and went by himself. That afternoon, as I was returning home, I saw David racing toward me on his bicycle waving a fish. I heard him yell, "Look, Dad, look at what I caught." At that very moment, I sadly realized that I had missed something very important that I could never reclaim. Children grow up too fast. I began noticing that my lay leaders thought nothing of missing an important board meeting, or even a Sunday worship service, to be away with one of their children for a football game.

I have come to understand that healthy congregations understand and appreciate when their pastors set an example of good parenting. Most elders don't begrudge their pastors spending quality time with their families. A pastor's leadership isn't just built on his communication skills and his commitment to the church. It is also dependent on his public example as a good husband and father. I don't regret giving my best to my church, but my family is also God's work. As I matured, I began to balance my priorities better.

The Results of Obedience

When I was a young Christian, I was advised to obey my parents even if it meant not going to church. Some even thought I should not return to school to study for the ministry until my parents agreed. If I had listened to them, I would never have been a pastor. God honored my obedience to Him. My mother was ashamed of my career choice until she visited me in Vermont while I was the pastor of the North Avenue Alliance Church. After observing the respect and love of the congregation for my gracious wife and me, her attitude changed. Her four beautiful and intelligent grandchildren also did a lot to influence her opinion of my decision to become a Christian and a pastor.

My mother said to me, "Albee, I regret my past opposition to you. You were right and I was wrong. I should not have tried to stop you." At every prayer meeting, during testimony time, she stood to her feet and proudly declared my virtues, "I want to thank God for my boy, Albee. He was always a good boy." At prayer time, she repeated aloud the same message to God. I became jittery about having a testimony or prayer time while she was around, but the people loved it and treated her like a queen. She took me aside after one prayer meeting, and asked me, "Albee, so how am I doing?" Before my mother returned to Brooklyn, she placed her trust in Jesus as her Messiah. She became a completed Jew before the God of our fathers.

Some might wonder how my mother could keep her promise to her father to die as a Jew and yet still believe in Jesus. The answer is very simple. Jesus is the Messiah of Israel and the Savior of the world. An ancient rabbi named Saul of Tarsus, an enemy of believers in Jesus who later became their advocate, wrote, "For he is not a Jew who is one outwardly. . . . But he is a Jew who is one inwardly; and circumcision is that which is of the heart, by the Spirit, not by the letter; and his praise is not from men, but from God" (Romans 2:28-29, NASB).

The day will come when my believing Jewish mother and I will walk on the streets of heaven together.

Seeking God's Guidance

A major theme in my preaching and counseling has always been to encourage people to seek and follow God's leading. God wants us to know His will for our lives, but one must believe that our welfare is God's highest concern. I have witnessed tragedies in the lives of some Christians who received divine guidance but then decided not to follow it.

One of my saddest memories occurred early in my ministry during the Vietnam War. A young man from the congregation informed me that God had called him to be a pastor. He applied to Nyack College to prepare himself for the ministry and was accepted for the fall term. I rejoiced with him, and together in prayer we consecrated his life for full-time ministry.

A few weeks later, he came to my study to tell me that he was going with his friends to enlist in the Marines to fight in

Vietnam before going on to college. I reminded him of the priority of God's call on his life. He said, "Don't worry, Pastor. After my enlistment is over, I will go to Nyack." I was not able to dissuade him.

After he completed his basic training, he came home on a short leave before shipping out to Vietnam. He was very sober as he sat down across from my desk. After a brief time of silence, he spoke with some difficulty. "Pastor," he said, "I made a mistake when I joined up. I should have followed God's guidance. I know that the Lord has forgiven me, but He has also revealed to me that I will not come home alive. I am now right with the Lord. Please tell my parents not to grieve because I will meet them in heaven."

Right after he arrived in Vietnam, he and his friends were placed in a helicopter along with a large supply of ammunition. They were being flown to a base camp under attack. While trying to land, they were fired upon by the enemy in the hills. The helicopter exploded and fell to the ground in pieces. Nothing was found of his body.

I do not believe for a minute that God was punishing him for not following through with His plan. God was leading him to college and the ministry to protect him from losing his life prematurely. We must seek God's guidance and then follow through, because it is always for our best interest. I know that the young man would want me to tell his story so that his example would help others to follow God's revealed will for their lives.

Acquiring Leadership Skills

General Maxwell Taylor said, "One expects a leader to demonstrate in his daily performance a thorough knowledge of his own job and further his ability to train his subordinates in their duties." In seminary, I was trained to be a chaplain type of pastor, not a leader. I needed to develop leadership skills. This became apparent to me on one occasion. I had suggested a board retreat. Everyone thought it was a great idea. I was excited for the opportunity to build a relationship with the men. I got all packed up and arrived at the retreat early along with my youth pastor. One of the men said, "Pastor, what are you doing here? This is a board retreat; it's not for pastors." I waited for the other men to defend my presence, but they all looked the other way. Instead of causing any trouble, we went home and made the best of the situation. I should not have allowed them to get away with it. In order to succeed as a pastor, I had to develop into an effective leader of men.

I committed myself to keep on acquiring new skills in my life. I have never lost my desire to learn. One day, Otto Gutwin, a project manager for IBM and one of my Vermont deacons, gently confronted me. "Pastor, you are a great preacher, but a very poor administrator."

"Otto, will you help me improve my skills?" I asked.

He agreed to tutor me in administration. He gave me a list of books on leadership, management and strategic planning. Otto encouraged the board to send me to seminars. The knowledge I had acquired during my academic days was inadequate for the rapid changes taking place in society. Each church I led demanded new understanding and additional skills. I asked the Lord to give me a desire to learn. Since then, I have taken a multitude of seminars and courses on all kinds of subjects.

As I acquired managerial skills, I began to understand what it takes to grow a church. First, I recognized the necessity that the pastor is the leader of the church. I decided to attempt to unify the elders behind me. Often board meetings were chaotic and filled with conflicts between the members. Everyone went home frustrated that nothing useful was accomplished.

Finally I understood the problem. I asked the board, "How many of you men believe the pastor should be the leader of the church?" Only half of the men raised their hands. The root problem was a divided board. If I tried to lead with a recommendation, half of the board would oppose me. If I did not take the lead by presenting a vision and recommendations, the other men complained about my lack of leadership. It was a lose/lose situation. It took me a long time to gain the leadership of the church. I stayed on for nine years working through the problems.

The second aspect of growing a church required the church to understand its purpose for existing. I invited the leadership and their wives to a dinner to discuss developing a mission statement for the church. I started the session with questions such as, "Why does our church exist? What is our purpose? What are we supposed to accomplish?" After a short discussion, we all realized we didn't have the foggiest idea what our mission was. We were unfocused. Later, the congregation was included in the process of brainstorming. Finally, we all agreed on a mission statement: "The mission of the North Avenue Alliance Church is to make disciples for Jesus Christ for the glory of God."

The next question before us was how to make disciples. We concluded that if we were to make an impact for Christ in Vermont, we had to become proactive. At a church growth seminar, Dr. Peter Wagner opened my eyes to the importance and potential of church growth principles. I learned that a church has three sources for growth: biological, conversion and transfer growth. We were doing poorly in all three areas.

Biological Growth

Our congregation's biological growth was a disappointment. Parents lamented over the loss of their children from the Christian faith. A local church that fails to win its children to the Christian faith has failed to achieve its main purpose for existing. I recommended to the board that we hire a youth pastor to reach our youth. The board claimed we could not afford one, and they turned down my request. Just about then, Dr. Roy Johnston, personnel director for The Christian and Missionary Alliance, phoned me to request that I take on Gordon Swenson as a missionary in training for two years. I had an idea that was a bit risky. I asked him to send me a telegram addressed to the congregation immediately, as we were going to have a congregational meeting that very night. I read it to the members. They voted to hire Gordon and his wife over the protests of some unhappy elders.

Later they came to appreciate him, because he influenced their own teenagers for Christ. Gordon was God's "Pied Piper" for teenagers. My own teenagers loved Gordon and followed him right into the kingdom of God. Everyone was sad to see Gordon and Pat leave for their missionary assignment in Indonesia. They left behind a turned-on youth fellowship and an active youth choir. Now whenever I visit the Vermont church, I see those same teenagers as adults sitting with their children and parents, worshiping God together.

Conversion Growth

Since we had little hope for transfer growth in static Vermont, we needed to find an effective strategy for evangelism.

One night I prayed, "Lord, I am not an evangelist, but Your Word says to a pastor, 'Do the work of an evangelist.' Teach me how to do it." The board agreed to pay my way to an evangelistic conference in Boston where I became acquainted with Evangelism Explosion.

Soon after I returned home from the evangelism conference, I recruited a team to go out with me every Thursday evening. Instantly, we began winning people to Christ. On one occasion, we visited a family who had attended our Christmas music program. The wife's heart was wide open to Christ. After she prayed, I asked the husband if he would receive eternal life through Christ. He replied, "Religion is all right for my wife; she isn't as well educated as I am." I knew he was in trouble that night.

He was completing his Ph.D. in botany at the university. I asked him, "So you are a scientist and you do research? Are you willing to pray, 'Oh God, if you really exist, convince me'?"

"Yes!" he replied. Since he was uncomfortable about praying, I did it for him.

A few weeks later, he came rushing into my office, very excited, exclaiming, "I know there is a God! I know there is a God!" I asked him how he found out. He explained that while studying a tiny desert flower under a magnifying glass, it hit him like a freight train there must be a creator of all this beauty. Then he said, "But I don't know if the creator is the God of the Bible."

"Well, why don't you ask Him?" I suggested. In a short time, he became a committed Christian. We don't have to argue intellectually to prove God; His existence is self-evident.

We began winning so many people to Christ in their homes that we were disappointed when people refused to receive Jesus at that very moment. Evangelism Explosion, however, taught me how to sow the seed of the gospel into the hearts of people and wait for the harvest.

One Sunday, Dr. Beth Hart, a professor at the University of Vermont, attended our services. As she was leaving, she insisted on telling me that she was an atheist. I asked her if she would object to a visit on campus so I could explain what she was rejecting. I promised we would not put any pressure on her to make a decision. She agreed to see us.

Over lunch, we shared the gospel point by point, making sure she understood it. As we promised, we did not ask her for a decision. Occasionally she came to church, claiming it was because she liked my Jewish sense of humor. As she was leaving a worship service one Sunday morning, I saw tears in her eyes, so I asked, "Are you ready to accept Jesus?"

"Yes!" She replied. In my office, she prayed to receive Jesus. Later she told me about her last class of the semester. She told her students, "In our first class together, I told you why I did not believe in God. Now I want to tell you why I do believe in Him." Beth then gave a thrilling testimony to those young people.

Karen Unsworth also appeared unwinnable. She came to see me about her mother's new faith in Christ. She was not pleased with the disruption in her family and informed me that she was a convinced atheist. She had done a great deal of research on atheism, filling up several notebooks with quotes and information that confirmed her viewpoint. She came to the services out of respect for her mother. If anyone seemed unreachable, Karen did.

One day she told me of a dream in which she had become a Christian and experienced indescribable joy, something she never felt before in her life. I said, "Your subconscious is smarter than you are." She laughed at the thought. I then said,

"I believe that God's Spirit is beginning to work in you and someday you will believe in Jesus. Whenever you are ready, call me day or night." A few months later, she informed me of her pending move to the Midwest, where she had accepted a job with a city planner. I didn't expect to hear from her again.

One morning at about 1 a.m. the phone rang, waking me up from a sound sleep. I heard a soft lady's voice saying, "I am ready."

I replied, "You must have the wrong number."

"No, I am ready!"

"Who is calling?"

"Pastor Runge, this is Karen Unsworth. I am ready to accept Jesus." We prayed together on the phone. When she returned to Vermont, I asked her what had happened. She told me her roommate had become a Christian at an evangelistic crusade and dragged her there with her. She experienced the conviction of the Holy Spirit. As soon as she returned to her apartment, she got out her notebooks and read all the arguments against the existence of God, but they made no sense to her, so she telephoned me.

Many times the biggest opponents of God become the strongest exponents of the faith. Such was the case of Karen.

Knowing how to move people to a decision is a necessary skill in business as well as in evangelism. For example, I knew an insurance agent who sold $4 million of new policies every year. At a lunch, I asked him, "Saul, you operate in a small territory with many other agents at work. How can you sell so much insurance with so many aggressive competitors?"

"Well, pastor, here's my secret," he answered. "Other agents may be good at only interesting people in buying insurance, while I know how to close the deal and sell a policy."

My training in Evangelism Explosion taught me how to encourage people to enter the kingdom of God. A young campus pastor at the University of Vermont attended my church. He was working with a promising group of non-Christian students. He lamented to me that another campus minister had moved in and led one of his students to Christ behind his back. He complained that he was sheep stealing.

I inquired, "Have you ever invited any of your Bible study group to accept Christ as their personal Savior?"

He replied defensively, "Well, no, they aren't ready yet."

To save him from further grief, I personally took the time and led every one of his students to Christ for him. The only way to know when a person is ready to accept Jesus is by asking him. Some of us have lost our nerve to ask for a decision. We are afraid of losing people. Fear is a lame excuse for our passivity and inaction. I think that the major reason behind the failure of the contemporary church in producing new Christians is timidity.

Various Strategies of Evangelism Are Important

Certainly the church needs to be innovative and create new strategies to reach people for Christ, but there is another side to this issue. Some older, discarded methods still work well. I recommended holding a week of revival meetings at North Avenue Alliance Church. I was informed that revival meetings were out-of-date, especially in Vermont. Since I persisted in my determination to invite an evangelist, the board went along with me. They were just waiting to show me how wrong I was.

The first time the evangelist preached he did it in Southern style. Shouting at the reserved Vermonters did not seem like a good idea. I began to fear that the crusade was going to be a disaster. By the end of the week, however, 125 people came down to the altar to receive Christ as their personal Savior. The gospel of Christ and the Word of God are relevant in every age. I look back with a great deal of satisfaction, remembering what God achieved through my feeble efforts. Reflecting on all those who came to know Christ in Burlington made all my sacrifices, struggles and efforts worthwhile.

Ungrounded Fears

During those early years of ministry, I feared going too far in the area of the miraculous. I wanted the Holy Spirit to use my messages to convict and convert the sinner. I longed to experience church growth through the power of God, but I did not want things to get beyond my control. If I could not understand something, I resisted it forcefully.

A group of new Christians from my congregation went to a retreat and came back excited. They claimed to have been filled with the Spirit. I immediately tried to settle them down with my theological perspective, which was somewhat anti-experience. I feared anything that even remotely appeared charismatic. Instead of rejoicing with them and encouraging them to walk in the Spirit, I drove them away with criticism.

Now that I know better, I thank God for not rejecting me. I put limits on the Spirit out of fear that I would be considered an extremist and a fanatic. I arrogantly limited the Holy Spirit as to what He could do within my congregation. Since He is the Spirit of grace, I was spared to see the day when I knew better. I thank God for His longsuffering with me. The Holy Spirit still continued to use me to win people to Christ and build up His Church.

A Ministry of Mentoring

While in Vermont, I began a ministry of mentoring young candidates for the ministry. Mentoring comes out of ancient Jewish practice. A rabbi selected a disciple to mentor and then ordained him as a rabbi. Saul of Tarsus sat at the feet of the great Rabbi Gamaliel and then became a rabbi himself. After his conversion, Barnabas mentored him. Later, Paul mentored Timothy and sent him out to teach what he learned. This is what Jesus did for His Jewish disciples. He taught them, ordained them and sent them forth in the world to spread His teaching.

One of the greatest needs of the kingdom of God is for mature mentors of young ministers. In the early days of the Church, there were no Bible schools or seminaries. Older and experienced pastors trained the younger pastors. Making disciples is the biblical basis for mentoring. When a young person enters the ministry with only a background in academic training, he still lacks the understanding of how to do the work in the ministry.

As one of my Jewish friends said of his son, who had acquired a Master of Business Administration degree, "He still has to learn the business from the ground up." The first day at work his educated son was given a broom and told to sweep up the stockroom. Eventually, the son became the president of the family firm. Learning is only theoretical until it is put to the test and refined by real life.

On-the-job training is required for most professions. For example, a physician is not ready to practice his profession with only academic learning. The last two years of medical school are dedicated to working in a hospital under careful tutelage. After graduation, the doctor is still required to work an addi-

I graduated from Toccoa Falls High School in 1949. Because of my conversion, no one from my family was there to share in the celebration. However, alone in my room, I sensed the approving presence of the Lord.

I went on to Bible college and proudly wore my one-and-only suit when I was invited to preach. One pastor's wife decided to do me a favor by pressing my pants on Saturday night with her newly purchased pressing machine. Neither of us knew that the suit was made of synthetic cloth that melted under high heat. It was an embarrassing end to my preaching suit.

From 1955 to 1965 I served as the resident pastor of the Beth Sar Shalom congregation. This picture, which includes my wife Lee and our first born, Ruth Robin, was taken in front of the Chosen People's Manhattan branch.

In 1967 we moved to Burlington, Vermont, to begin an eight-year ministry at the North Avenue Alliance Church. My first task was to counsel a young widow who had just lost her husband in the crash of his jet fighter. While in Burlington, I began learning how to grow a multi-staff church.

My father always made fun of Aunt Rose left, and her chicken soup. She was so cheap, he said, that she would only dip a chicken in the hot water to give it a little flavor. Aunt Rose was the best friend of my mother (right).

The Omaha Gospel Tabernacle. Prior to my coming in 1975, the church had gone through a major split leaving behind a discouraged people. I prayed desperately for wisdom to understand the situation and to know what to do about it. In 1978, the congregation sold their downtown building and relocated to a new facility on 25 acres of land beside the interstate. See next page. (Dr. Francis Grubbs is on the right.)

The church was later renamed Christ Community Church of The Christian and Missionary Alliance. My vision for the congregation became a reality, and in the process I learned the power of faith goals that depend on the resources of God and not ours.

In 1999, Larry and Barbara Boss were my hosts in Poland. The younger missionaries and pastors appreciated the legacy of six decades of experience in the ministry.

While in Poland, I also had the opportunity to preach (through an interpreter) to university students from Poland, Russia, Ukraine, Belarus and Lithuania. These young people were among the elite of their nations. I was deeply touched by their hunger for the Word of God and their desire for godly counsel. The student on the left is from Russia.

My first missionary tour was to Indonesia. The picture above includes students from the Jakarta Bible College. On a second trip to Jakarta some years later, I presented a seminar on Christian leadership at the Alliance Seminary. Dr. Tomatala, President of the Seminary, presents me with flowers and a letter of appreciation. Retirement was not the end of ministry for Lee and me. Rather, it was the beginning of a challenge that would take us worldwide as a Minister-at-Large with The Christian and Missionary Alliance.

In January of 2000, we were invited to minister in South America. In Buenos Aires, Argentina, I preached to a messianic assembly where David Constance interpreted for me.

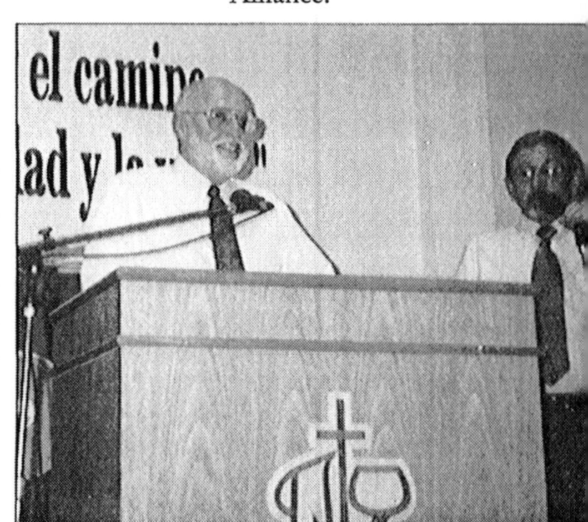

While the church was under construction, every Monday morning Lee and I went for breakfast at a nearby motel overlooking the site. We watched with great interest as our dream church took shape. It was difficult to leave this beloved congregation when the time came.

The expanded facilities became a reality through the power of the Lord Jesus Christ. There is now an average of 2,700 worshipers in the morning services and 2,000 in Sunday school.

Our next ministry took us to Edmonton, Alberta, Canada to lead the congregation of Beulah Alliance Church. Once again, the church was in transition. In 1987 we purchased ten acres of prime land a few blocks from the world-famous West Edmonton Mall.

I enjoyed preaching the Word of God and serving and loving the congregation. Over 2,000 people worship in the new facility.

In January of 2000, Lee and I ministered to the missionaries of The Christian and Missionary Alliance in Argentina.

I have said many times that it was Lee's faithful love and prayers that enriched my life by giving me support and security in our shared ministries. Approaching fifty years of marriage, we are still serving the Lord together.

In August of 2000, our entire family gathered together for a reunion where we compiled our family's life purpose statement: "To glorify God by enlarging the kingdom of God beginning with our own family and by reaching out compassionately to the world as significant Christian leaders."

tional year or two under the supervision of older, experienced physicians. To become a specialist, another four to five years are added to his training on the job.

A minister, however, is expected to begin his career right out of Bible school or seminary. In no way am I belittling academic preparation! It is necessary, but school learning by itself is incomplete.

Gordon and Pat Swenson were my first candidates for mentoring. Interestingly, they are still active in youth ministries in Indonesia. They are now influencing the youth of an entire national denomination. When I visited them in Indonesia, I realized how valuable they had become to the kingdom of God. I am very proud of Gordon and Pat.

I learned a great deal in the process of mentoring the young, especially about spiritual giftedness. Before I left Vermont to take on another church, I hired Dick Lawson, another missionary candidate, to be our youth pastor. Right from the beginning of our association, he was honest with me: "Youth ministry is not where I am most gifted; I am looking for an assistant pastor's position." I disregarded what he said because I did not fully understand gifts at that time. Dick worked very hard and did an excellent job with the youth, but it was not until after I left the church that he demonstrated his major giftedness. Dick became the interim pastor and put his exceptional gifts of ministry into practice. The congregation prospered under his leadership. Dick and Jo Lawson also went to Indonesia. The field chairman told me that they were among the very best missionaries in the field. I was heartsick to hear of the accident that took Jo Lawson's life. Dick is still serving Christ faithfully. I will always appreciate his integrity, strength and faith. He is one of my shining stars.

I have had the privilege of mentoring a number of young pastors and missionaries down through the years who are now serving Christ in various parts of the world. They are a great joy for me.

Knowing When to Leave

In my tenth year in Vermont, I wondered if my ministry was completed. A fellow pastor said, "When you start asking that question, your ministry at the church is coming to a conclusion." My vision and burden for the church weren't there anymore. My sense of responsibility for the church's future was gone. God was preparing me to move on to another challenge. The church wasn't quite ready to sell their facility and build a new church. It took them ten years after I left to finally make their move. All God wanted from me was to lay down a good foundation for their future.

CHAPTER NINE

Watching God at Work

"For I am the LORD, your God,
who takes hold of your right hand
and says to you, Do not fear;
I will help you.
Do not be afraid, O worm Jacob,
O little Israel,
for I myself will help you," declares the LORD,
your Redeemer, the Holy One of Israel.
(Isaiah 41:13-14)

While I was struggling to know God's direction for my future, Dr. Keith Bailey, the acting superintendent of the Western District, phoned me. "Al, there is a leading congregation in Omaha that has just experienced a serious split. I believe you are God's man to restore that church."

Lee was reluctant to leave her friends and the congregation she loved. The move would not be easy for my children either because they loved Vermont. They learned to ski in the winter and hike through the Green Mountains in the summer. We had a pleasant life in beautiful Vermont. However, my wife's strongest motivation has always been to support my ministry, so she reluctantly came along with me to size up the situation. People warned us against going to Omaha; nevertheless, Lee and I arrived in Omaha to candidate for the church. The opportunity didn't look very promising.

The Tabernacle was located in the declining downtown area, a few blocks from where rioting had taken place the previous summer. I was also told that prostitutes occasionally walked by the church, propositioning some churchgoers. On top of all of those disadvantages, the old facilities were run-down and unattractive.

The pastor who had left was also popular with the remaining members of the congregation, so when he accepted the call to a newly formed congregation in the city, his decision was looked upon as a threat to the future of the Tabernacle. A number of younger families left the Tabernacle to join the new church. In spite of the poor outlook, my wife and I fell in love with the hurting congregation. We decided to accept the challenge to become their senior pastor if the board gave us a unanimous call before we left the city.

After receiving the call and just before we left for Omaha, God spoke to me through His Word, clarifying my function for the Tabernacle: "You will be called Repairer of Broken Walls, Restorer of Streets with Dwellings. . . . The children born . . . will yet say in your hearing, 'This place is too small for us; give us more space to live in' " (Isaiah 58:12; 49:20).

The Spirit of God was predicting how He was going to use me at the Tabernacle. During the difficult days, those verses gave me the faith and courage to carry on.

Serving a demoralized congregation wasn't easy on us. Many who had stayed with the church were still loyal to their former pastor and were upset over the conflict. For over a year and a half, significant families continued to leave the church. Our entire deacon board left, one by one. We falsely presumed that all the people remaining at the Tabernacle would stay and support our leadership. We could not have been more wrong. During the first year, many people told me, "We have nothing against you personally, since we don't know you. We are leaving the church because we don't approve of the way our pastor was treated by the board."

I was consistently being asked, "Do you think our church can survive?" I remember one special worship service. As I sat on the platform looking over the congregation waiting for my turn to preach, I could see the despair in the faces of the people. Suddenly, I began feeling in my own heart the pain of the congregation. The feeling was so strong, I had to hold back the tears. I then promised the Lord that I would never hurt His people. If the day came that I was being forced out, I would go quietly. I resolved never to be a party to a church split.

I informed the congregation, "I am going to address the problem of the church split only this one time, and then we must put it behind us." I then spoke to them from Ephesians 4:30-32:

> And do not grieve the Holy Spirit of God, with whom you were sealed for the day of redemption. Get rid of all bitterness, rage and anger, brawling and slander, along with every form of malice. Be kind and compassionate to one another, forgiving each other, just as in Christ God forgave you.

My main point was simple. If we please the Holy Spirit, we will have a great future ahead of us, but if we grieve Him, we will lose God's blessing. So I asked them to put away bitterness from their hearts toward those who had left them. I exhorted them not to criticize anyone and to forgive those who had hurt them.

The circumstances were not very encouraging. Some wondered out loud if the glory had departed from their once great church. I kept assuring the people that the Lord never forsakes

His people. Every message I gave was full of optimism and faith for the future. After a while the congregation began to believe with me that there was a future for the church.

Once the congregation adopted a positive faith attitude, there was no limit to the outpouring of God's blessings. Even while the Omaha Gospel Tabernacle was still at its seedy downtown location, the congregation grew from 450 to 1,200 people, exceeding all the past attendance records. The Spirit of God works actively in an atmosphere of unity, faith and love.

Our Lord did not mislead us. Lee and I were given the privilege of watching God at work. One of my major prayers has always been, "Lord, lead me to a place where You intend to do a mighty work." The invisible hand of God accomplished the success we began experiencing.

There was some major strength left in the Omaha Gospel Tabernacle. The people who remained were loyal and possessed a deep spiritual commitment to the evangelization of Omaha. The remaining lay leaders desired to renew and relocate the church in the growing area of the city. They were willing to follow the leadership of their new senior pastor. I was happy to have such an opportunity to lead a church in growth.

Continuously Learning

The board was generous and wise in providing me with the opportunity to take many study seminars. My first and foremost task was to preach God's Word clearly and persuasively. As my ministry developed, I needed to acquire additional skills. So I took advantage of continuing education in counseling, in preaching, in exegesis of Scripture, church administration and church growth.

About every five to seven years, I make an effort to get retrained in preaching, because audiences' interests are always changing. For example, in the 1950s, I was taught not to use personal illustrations because people might think I was egocentric. Today people want to know about their pastor's spiritual pilgrimage, his struggles and victories. A pastor who shares himself is viewed as an authentic person with whom ordinary people can relate.

I was also taught in seminary to expound on theology without the use of too many stories; however, a contemporary congregation learns theology best through illustrations. Jesus, the master Teacher, taught spiritual truth through parables. Good storytelling holds people's interest in a sermon. There were times when I repeated an illustration in a totally different message, yet some people complained that I was repeating an old message. They had forgotten the exposition, but remembered the illustration. I often wished I could be like a soloist who sings the same songs more than once and still delights a congregation.

When I was a seminary student, one of my professors said every pastor should acquire an expertise beyond preaching. Over the years I attempted to become knowledgeable about church growth. I sought to understand church dynamics. To acquire that skill, I studied management, organizational development and conflict management. Those skills enabled me to achieve meaningful church growth.

I owe a special debt of gratitude to Dr. Peter Wagner. He contributed much to the successes of my ministry. In Church Growth 101, he explained that his main objective for his students was to develop their church-growth eyes. He used the illustration of the cockpit of a 767. If we were to look at the instrument panel with all its switches and indicators, everything would confuse us. A pilot trained to fly a 767 enters the cockpit, and without much thought, does all the right procedures, presses all the right buttons and flies the plane thousands of miles away to the right destination. He does it all without a moment of confusion because he has trained 767 eyes. Omaha was an opportunity for me to put into practice what I had learned.

Building a Team

At the Omaha church I was so busy at first trying to stop the exiting of good people that I hardly had the time to do anything else. Yet I knew that I had to come up with a strategy to rebuild the Tabernacle, so I began praying for wisdom to understand the situation and what to do about it. The Tabernacle needed innovative ministries to meet the spiritual and social needs of people.

My first task was to build a staff of gifted pastors. No profession is as demanding as the Christian ministry. A pastor is expected to be an excellent theologian, a wise counselor, an expert biblical expositor, a clear communicator, an able administrator and a skillful politician. Since no one person can be good in all the skills expected of him, he must develop and manage a team of professional and lay ministers who will equip others to do the work of the ministry. God calls and gives specialized ministry gifts to people. I have found that people placed in the ministry according to their giftedness produce growth naturally in a church and are happy doing it.

I started out by evaluating the staff I had inherited. One staff member was demoralized over the split in the church. This was understandable because in just one week he had lost two-thirds of his Sunday school teachers to the other church. He loved and respected the former pastor, and in his heart he believed that the pastor had been unfairly treated. In my judgment, it was best for him and the Tabernacle if he would find another ministry.

At the next board meeting, he announced to the lay leaders, "God has called me to continue on in my present position." Who can argue against God? Certainly not me! I understood his hesitation to leave, so we allowed him to stay on with the condition that he would try out various other ministries. He taught the college class for a period of time. Those young adults were thrilled with him. Everyone, including himself, was happy. Later he accepted an invitation to teach at a Christian college. Today he is the head of his department. In time, he recognized that I was only trying to help him find God's special place of service for his life. We can't expect success unless we are doing the job God has assigned to us.

Too often good people are placed in the wrong positions. Misplacing staff creates frustration for everyone, including the staff member, as well as hindering the growth of a congregation. Sometimes even a right choice turns out badly. I had recruited a staff member who possessed an unusual gift of compassion, which made him an ideal minister of pastoral care. When he spoke comfort to a hurting person, it was as if Jesus Himself was doing the talking. When he hugged someone, there was a real sense of the presence of Christ. He conveyed the genuine love of Jesus. Unfortunately, his ambition was to preach, and speaking took him away from his assigned duties. Even his best friends admitted that when he preached, time stood still for them. He also insisted that he was a gifted administrator, but every organizational task assigned to him fell apart.

I thought for our mutual benefit and the good of the church, that it was time for a heart-to-heart talk. I explained how much he meant to the congregation and me. I enumerated the reasons why he should stick to the job description for which he was gifted. I tried to be honest as well as tactful with him, but I failed. Reacting angrily, he resigned to become a senior pastor of a small church.

More than twenty years have passed by. All along his way, people affirmed his special gift of mercy, while telling him of his lack of preaching and administrative skills. If he had only recognized his true giftedness! It is just as important to know the gifts we lack as well as the gifts we have. One of the major ways to identity our gift is by the confirmation of the body of Christ.

In my search for anointed men and women to serve on the pastoral team, I looked for people who were already demonstrating their ministry gifts successfully. I began my search to find a pastor to lead and develop the ministry of evangelism. While on a missionary trip in the Far East, I met Tom Stebbins, a former missionary to Vietnam, serving temporarily as the pastor of the Hong Kong International Church. I was impressed with his evangelistic zeal and efforts in promoting Evangelism Explosion in the churches of the city. I asked him to consider working with us on our pastoral team, and after he completed his overseas assignment, he accepted my invitation.

Tom Stebbins did an outstanding job. He influenced the leaders of the church to participate in evangelism. The church board decided that in order to serve in leadership, everyone had to take at least one semester of Evangelism Explosion training. In addition, Tom organized forty evangelistic teams of three members each that went out weekly to share the good news of Jesus. He established and administrated a yearly evangelism training session for pastors and lay people of other churches. Tom's influence reached around the world. He traveled to Europe, Africa and Asia conducting evangelism training seminars. Today he heads up Evangelism Explosion International. Much of the success of the Omaha Tabernacle that came to be known as Christ Community Church arose out of his ministry of mobilizing the congregation for evangelism.

Training Young Pastors

In spite of the many demands on me as a senior pastor, I think my most significant contribution to the kingdom of God was recruiting inexperienced young people. Tom Mangham, a missionary in training, applied to become my youth pastor. I interviewed him at an Alliance Council. I said, "Tom, if you can promise me that you will work hard and give me your best, I will take a chance on you. If you let me down, it will hurt my leadership with my church board. I want you to pray about it tonight with your wife and tell me tomorrow of your decision."

The next day Tom assured me that they would give me their best. Tom and Barbara did far more than I had a right to expect. My own rebellious son, Peter, came to Christ under his leadership. Today the vast majority of the young people he shepherded are still active in the Christian faith.

Tom and Barbara are now hard-working and effective missionaries in the Far East. When I went to visit them, Tom took two weeks off to guide me around and be my interpreter. Recently I have advised them to slow down—they aren't as young as they used to be. Some of my dearest and closest friends are the young people I had the privilege of training for the ministry.

The Power of Faith Goals

I learned about missionaries using faith goals successfully overseas. I believed that this principle of setting faith goals was applicable anywhere, for everyone, and at any time. Since faith goals succeed on the mission field, why not in North America? I discovered how God honors faith goals in church growth. The Word of God supports this principle: "By faith [they] conquered kingdoms, performed acts of righteousness, obtained promises, shut the mouths of lions, quenched the power of fire, escaped the edge of the sword, from weakness were made strong, became mighty in war, put foreign armies to flight" (Hebrews 11:33-34, NASB).

An opportunity for me to recommend faith goals came at the 1978 Alliance Council in Birmingham, Alabama. The president reported that our denomination was closing more churches each year than it was planting new ones. I was appointed to the Council committee that reviewed his report. I initiated the motion that we recommend to the General Council to adopt a faith goal to double our North American constituency in ten years. The denominational leadership representatives on the committee were dubious about the motion and objected. "Where are we going to get the money, the land and the pastors?"

I replied, "It is a faith goal; we will trust God to provide the resources."

Council voted for it overwhelmingly and ten years later we rejoiced over what God did for our denomination.

Faith goals differ from realistic goals. Both are needed and they work well together. Most organizations set reasonable and measurable goals based on careful projections that take into account the present and predictable resources. A church's strategic plan must adopt faith goals that depend on the resources of God along with developing practical ordinary goals before any action is taken. I asked the congregation, "What would you do for God's glory if you had all the resources necessary to do them?" At a brainstorming session, all kinds of suggestions for strategies came up.

At the end of the meeting, I was overwhelmed. I asked the people, "Do you have any idea how much money these ideas will cost us? Can we trust God for these resources?" I then asked for a motion stating that if God provided the means, we would use them to accomplish our mission. After a positive vote, I prayed something like this, "Father, Your children have expressed their desire to do these great things for You, but we don't have the resources to accomplish them. If You give us what we need, we will do them for Your glory."

Before I left, the congregation accomplished what they desired to do. Faith goals work if the motivation is to serve and glorify God. When a congregation sees and accepts a God-given vision for their own, they will never lack the resources to achieve it.

Search for a Better Site

After the Omaha congregation began to outgrow the facilities, it was time to form a land-search committee. For a number of years, the leadership of the church had attempted to relocate the congregation in the western part of the city without much success. The church had purchased seven acres of land there, but three of the acres were in a gully and difficult to use. They would provide only limited parking that would accommodate a congregation of 500 worshipers. The vision that we had was for a much larger church. After the vision was laid out and a strategic plan was accepted and put into action, the congregation began to grow rapidly in the downtown location. It soon became apparent that our new location was inadequate to fulfill our purposes.

So we began a new search. Land was extremely expensive and a large enough parcel of land seemed impossible to find. We then discovered a very large parcel of vacant land adjacent to a major interstate freeway that went through the western part of the city. The Mutual of Omaha Insurance Company owned it. Three of us—Jack Bishop, Bill Alford and myself—looked the land over and walked on it. It was a perfect site. I suggested that we pray and claim it for the Lord.

I prayed, "Lord, we claim this land to build a great church for Your glory that will bless this community for generations to come." I ended my prayer in Jesus' name.

I contacted the real estate agent for the insurance company. He replied, "Sorry, many businesses and even a church wanted to buy it, but the board of directors voted not to sell it but to keep it in reserve as a future investment."

I wasn't willing to take no for an answer, so I composed a four-page letter sharing my vision for a church on their site and sent it to the board of directors of the insurance company. A few weeks later the real estate agent called back and said, "I can't explain it, but the directors are asking you to make a bid for twenty-six acres of their land. They will sell no more or no less of the land."

Trying to estimate the value of the land was beyond my imagination. I decided that there was nothing to lose by offering a low bid of $250,000 for the twenty-six acres of land.

The real estate agent replied, "There is no way that I am going to take that ridiculously low bid back to the board."

"Listen," I insisted, "you have to! They asked for a bid, and we have given it. Do you work for the board or do they work for you?"

Humanly speaking, I expected to be turned down. Sure enough, the board did—but then they made a counter offer of $540,000, take it or leave it. I acted immediately, even without asking our elders for their approval, and accepted their offer. I have learned that whenever we move in God's will, nothing can stop us.

At the congregational meeting called to decide the purchase of the property, an antagonistic woman stood up and with deep emotion demanded, "Who is going to pay for all this land?"

I responded, "You are, or don't vote for it. I will do my part, but I don't have the resources to do it all by myself."

By secret ballot, the congregation voted by over ninety-one percent to purchase the land. As far as I know, we lost only one family in the move.

Raising Money

Two contractors wanted to buy our other piece of land in the gully. We auctioned it off for $250,000. We needed a lot more money to build the new facilities, and at the time, I lacked the skill of raising money. Without the necessary financial support, the church could not relocate to the better part of the city and add the facilities necessary for church growth.

When it came to raising the amounts of money needed to accomplish the task of relocating the church, I knew I needed help. I did what I usually do when I am uncertain: I prayed for guidance. The Lord clearly revealed to me that since I didn't know how to raise money, it was necessary to hire those who had the ability to guide us through a stewardship campaign. I knew there would be strong opposition to such a suggestion. The fund-raising organization we had interviewed wanted $50,000 for their fee. This amount did not include all the other expenses of the campaign such as advertising and a complimentary churchwide banquet. I foresaw the reactions—"Let's give the money to missions instead" and "We can do it ourselves." In the recent past, before I became their pastor, the church had already tried to raise pledges of $500,000 by themselves to go and build a new church on their seven acres of land, but they had failed.

I stood boldly before the congregation one Sunday morning and said, "I take seriously the commandment that says, 'Thou shall not take the name of the Lord thy God in vain.' So what I am about to tell you is laying my ministry on the line. The Lord has told me to tell you to hire Resource Services to help us raise money to build His church. I realize that I am laying my head on the chopping block, and if this doesn't work out, I will lose my credibility with you and it will end my ministry as your pastor."

No one stirred in the congregation; I had gotten their attention and had silenced the opposition. Over the years, I have listened to people who claimed that the Lord had spoken to them, but their projects failed. Such actions do not bear witness of God's wisdom or holiness. They lost their credibility with me. However, there were others who demonstrated over time that God really does communicate with them. What they said in the name of the Lord happened. My greatest desire is to be a genuine servant of Jesus, so what I said to the church that day I said in great seriousness and fear. Over the years I have learned to pay attention to His gentle voice.

The Lord did not mislead me. He had everything under control. A few men surprised me by deciding to pay the $50,000 fee. The very next week, I reported their gift to the congregation. I was able to announce that the fee would not come out of missionary or general funds.

The advertisements and mailings went out on time. Everything was ready to go as planned. About 800 people were coming to the banquet on a Sunday evening, which was to be the highlight of the campaign. Everything was going well in our stewardship drive until the night before the banquet. I heard on the radio that a severe blizzard was going to hit Omaha by midnight. This storm would close down the city so that no one could be at the banquet.

I knew how important the all-church banquet was to the campaign, so I fell to my knees and told God, "Lord, if this blizzard hits our city and our banquet is cancelled, I will never, never, never again tell anyone that You speak to me. How would I know? Lord, not only do we need the banquet, but we also need an additional week of good weather to gather up the pledges."

I did not pray out of a rebellious spirit, but out of genuine concern not to deceive anyone or to misuse the name of God. I opened my Bible to a verse that spoke to me. "He who watches over Israel will neither slumber nor sleep" (Psalm 121:4) I got up from my knees and said, "Since you are awake all night, I am going to sleep."

The next morning, I got up and looked out the window. There was no snow on the ground. The radio announcer said the storm was right outside of Omaha and would hit the city by 10 that morning. Later that day, the weather report told us that the blizzard would hit about 3 in the afternoon, but it never came. After our successful evening banquet, while driving home, I heard two men speaking on the radio. One said it had been a freak storm. It came to the outskirts of the city and stopped as if it had hit a force field. The blizzard then turned 90 degrees and went south. I had a hallelujah time in my car. The stewardship drive was a great success.

Building the church of God takes a lot of miracles. The Bible tells us, "Unless the LORD builds the house, its builders labor in vain" (Psalm 127:1). The greatest lesson I have learned in the ministry is that when a church follows the Lord's will, nothing is impossible.

Along with a God-given vision, we needed to develop a practical step-by-step plan. The pledges enabled us to estimate the amount the congregation was able and willing to invest in the project over a three-year period along with the understanding that a stewardship drive would take place every three years until the entire project was completed and paid for. We resolved to borrow only what our present congregation would be able to pay off in fifteen years. We chose to plan the entire church facilities with all the future additions, but to build only what we could afford at that time. All other future extensions were to be built debt-free. The bank loaned us $1.8 million dollars on the basis of the pledges.

Testing My Motivation

The Omaha Gospel Tabernacle was soon to be renamed The Christ Community Church. Lee and I identified with the congregation. They had become our family and our lives. Every Monday morning we went to a coffee shop and sat by a window from which we watched our dream church being built. We expected to be there until we went to heaven.

Finally we had arrived! I was the pastor of a fast-growing church that at the time was the largest in The Christian and Missionary Alliance. The alumni association of Toccoa Falls College voted me the man of the year. The publishers of the "Who's Who in the Religious Life of America" wanted to list me. The editors of a popular leadership magazine asked to write up the story of the amazing restoration of an older, declining church. To top it all off, I was elected to the Board of Managers of my denomination. I felt that I had found my life's ministry.

However, questions kept coming to my mind: What was my real motivation for serving Jesus? Was it out of selfish ambition or for the glory of God? Would I be available to leave and take on another difficult challenge? As the inner struggle unfolded, I sought the wisdom of God. *What should I do?* Needing to be alone with God, I went to the balcony of the new sanctuary. I sat there silently for some time reflecting over all the love, efforts and planning my wife and I had invested for the church's success. Could I walk away from such a once-in-a-lifetime opportunity if God asked me to do it?

My struggle all boiled down to my primary motivation for serving Jesus. I reflected over the conversation between the resurrected Jesus and Peter on the shore of Lake Galilee. There was only one issue with Jesus; it was the issue of love. Three times He asked Peter, "Do you love me?" Peter answered positively each time; thereupon Jesus gave Peter a mandate to care for His sheep. (See John 21:15-18.) The Greek text is eye-opening. The first two times Jesus used the Greek word *agape,* signifying the highest form of love known to man, divine love. All three times, Peter replied with the Greek word *philos,* brotherly love, an acknowledgment of a lesser love, human love. The third time Jesus lowered His expectation and asked Peter, "Do you really love me with human love?"

"Yes!" replied Peter, "You know all things, you know I love you." Jesus accepted the best that Peter could give Him at the time.

The question before me was did I love Jesus enough to let go of my dreams, walk away and take on another assignment? I began to understand that the church belonged to Jesus, not to me. God had done it all. All the glory belonged to Him. I let go of the church and turned it back to the care of the Lord.

I then spoke to my Lord Jesus, "Lord, I remember the day I had no potential to serve You. When I wandered the streets of Brooklyn alone, You called me and gave me wonderful opportunities to see You at work. It was You, not me, O Lord, who healed and restored this shattered church. Lord, these are Your people, not mine. I turn them all back over to You."

God had wonderful blessings in store for me that I would have missed had I not accepted the invitation of the Beulah Alliance Church in Edmonton, Alberta, Canada, to become its senior pastor. Having my answer from God, I walked out of the new church. I sensed the comfort of the Lord as He walked by my side. Many of our friends did not understand why we had to accept another call. Some even became angry with us for leaving them.

In my last sermon, I told the congregation, "Many of you like to call yourself 'Rungeites.' If you insist on wearing that label, let me tell you how true Rungeites behave. Their first and ultimate loyalty is to Christ and not to me. They remain loyal to their church. You who love me will disappoint me and make my ministry fruitless if you leave the church because we are not here anymore."

I then asked Tom Stebbins, my assistant pastor, to come to the platform. Along with the elders, I laid my hands on his head and prayed God's blessing on him, as he would have to lead the congregation through the interim period.

At our farewell service a lady said to me, "When you came, I was distressed to hear that they called a Jew to be our pastor, but since then I have come to respect you and love the Jews."

I view those years at Omaha with a great deal of satisfaction. Not only has the church grown to over 2,600 worshipers and 2,000 in the Sunday school, but also the congregation is now giving over $1 million a year to missions under the capable leadership of my successor, Pastor Bob Thune.

God had also used the past unpleasant rupture of the congregation of the old Omaha Gospel Tabernacle to bring greater growth for the kingdom of God. Today there are two strong churches in Omaha with a combined attendance of over 6,000 people. What they could not do together, they have done separately.

I wasn't completely sure of it then, but I now know it was God's time for us to leave. He had other tasks for us to accomplish. His assignment for us in Omaha was completed.

I wondered if my success at Omaha was just a one-time occurrence, or if God had endowed me with a gift that brings healing to a wounded church. From this point in time, I can reflect back on all the churches I pastored and acknowledge that God had called me to be a "Repairer of Broken Walls" (Isaiah 58:12).

CHAPTER TEN

Time to Move On

Now the LORD said to Abram, "Go forth from your country, and from your relatives . . . to the land which I will show you." (Genesis 12:1, NASB)

I had sent out my résumé to all the Alliance District Superintendents. Thirteen opportunities to candidate opened up for us within weeks. My first invitation was from Beulah Alliance Church in Edmonton, Alberta. I was very impressed with the history of the church. During its sixty-five years of existence, it had planted six healthy congregations in and around the Edmonton area. Beulah Alliance is called the mother church of Western Canada for good reason. The board honored me with an invitation to become their senior pastor.

When the opportunity came to candidate in Edmonton, I did it with some apprehension. I had been attending the Bergen Street Tabernacle in Brooklyn, New York as a teenager when a new pastor came from Toronto, Canada. It must have been a severe cultural shock for him to come from the proper and conservative Ontario to oversee our Brooklyn congregation. I don't think he was prepared to pastor people like me. He warned me never to try to pastor a Canadian church. "You will never make it with Canadians."

The move was the hardest on my wife because we left two of our children and two grandchildren behind in Omaha. "They live so far away," Lee lamented. "What good is it to be a grandmother with no grandchildren?" For company while I was busy in the church, she purchased a "Yorkie," a little dog with a big attitude. For hours the dog slept on Lee's lap while she read. What that dog lacked in size she made up in devotion. No mistake about it—she was my wife's dog. She only tolerated me.

Generosity is the word that best describes the congregation in Edmonton. They purchased half of my house, which enabled me to build up some equity. They gave us an excellent salary and started us on a good pension plan. They not only appreciated Lee and me, but they also defended us against the few but persistent chronic complainers.

The Importance of Listening to People

Just before we arrived on the scene, the church had purchased forty-two acres of farmland just outside the city limits of Edmonton for relocating their facilities. The Winterburn property was hastily purchased because of its availability at a price the church was able to pay at the time. The elders were considering borrowing $3 million from the bank. One of the reasons the elders called me to be their pastor was because of my experience in relocating a major church. Everything seemed ready to proceed with the relocation.

In seminary I was taught to preach, teach and talk to people, but not how to listen. Yet listening is a most important skill for the ministry. Over time I learned its importance to a successful ministry. My wife and I began systematically visiting the active members of the church in order to get acquainted. During our conversations with each family, we asked the same question, "What do you think of moving our church to the Winterburn property?" We were alarmed to hear prominent church people saying over and over again, "When the church moves, we will not be going along." Many felt the site was too far away and unsafe for winter travel.

I found out that after the new site was purchased, about 200 people had left the church in silent protest. Even two elders who voted to buy it told me they were compelled to go along with the decision in order to present a united front with the leadership to the congregation.

At the next board meeting I revealed what I was hearing and expressed concern that there might be as much as one-third of the congregation not behind the project. I asked the board, "Can we afford the move with the loss of a third of our members?" Obviously the answer was negative.

I was put through an intense inquisition. Some of the elders doubted my evaluation. Finally, I said, "Look, I am new here; give me time to build up my credibility in order to lead the congregation into such a major move." The project was put on hold for two years. Everyone settled down and began working together to build up the congregation in their downtown location.

About a year later, we invited two couples over for dinner. They bluntly expressed deep disappointment with me. They asserted that ninety-eight percent of the people wanted to move the church to Winterburn as soon as possible. They blamed me for stopping it because I had listened to a few unimportant dissidents.

"Well," I replied, "if that is true, we should move the church, but first we need to determine fairly the viewpoint of the congregation." I recommended to the board the formation of a committee of three members to create a survey. The committee's mandate was to formulate a fair questionnaire that no one could criticize. The survey was created and then distributed on three consecutive Sundays. The results showed that seventy-four percent of the congregation was not in favor of moving the church to Winterburn.

At the next board meeting, the elders sat around the table in silent shock. One strong supporter of the relocation asked me, "How could we have been so wrong?" I explained that the church was suffering from "group blindness." There were many groups with various viewpoints in our church. Our elders made up only one group, ninety percent of whom wanted to move the church to the new site. Communication between the groups had broken down. The elders and their friends talked only among themselves, building up in their minds the false impression that everyone was in support of the move. Other groups felt intimidated into silence by the warning that to oppose the relocation was the same as opposing God's will.

A short time later, we discovered that all of this aggravation suffered by the congregation was pointless: the city had just incorporated the Winterburn property into its jurisdiction and refused to rezone it for a church. We could not build on it even if we had the money to do it.

The congregation had paid out $1.25 million for unusable land that no one else wanted to buy. The biggest challenge facing me was finding a way to restore the congregation's confidence in their future.

There were other uncertainties that needed to be resolved before we could think about relocation. The congregation was divided into three factions. One group did not desire the church to grow any bigger. A second group wanted the church to divide and plant a daughter church in the West End, and the third group wanted to relocate the entire church from the declining downtown.

The Importance of Listening to God

Even with all the growth we were having downtown, I lost all interest in relocating the church. I wondered why. Perhaps God wasn't in the move. I thought, *After all, God doesn't expect all His churches to be large with huge staffs.*

Finally, I went to the Source of all wisdom and asked the Lord to give me an insight into my resistance. I prayed, "Lord, why am I so reluctant to relocate this church? Has Your Spirit put a check in my heart not to go ahead or what?"

God clearly spoke to me: "You don't want to pay the price!"

I responded, "Oh Lord, if my only reason is that I don't want to pay the price, I will pay the price whether I feel like it or not."

I had good reasons to be satisfied with the status quo. The church was growing again. My life was peaceful, working along with easygoing elders who were men of integrity. I was enjoying the best salary I had ever had. There wasn't any opposition or conflict to overcome except the one about relocating. I thought, *Why complicate my life with another church relocation project?* The magnitude of such a move would demand a lot of hard work and sacrifice on my part. I understood that at the completion of a church relocation very few pastors stay long enough to enjoy the fruits of their labors. Usually it is the succeeding pastor that gets all the recognition and rewards from the sacrifices and hard work of his predecessor. Within myself, I thought the effort wasn't worth it.

Through another survey, we discovered that most of the congregation was not opposed to relocating the church to a site within the city; they just did not want to move their church ten miles outside the city limits.

In order to proceed in moving the church to a more suitable site within the city, the congregation first had to forgive the mistake of running ahead of the Lord by spending all their available money on unusable property. Secondly, they would be asked for millions of dollars more to buy another site and build larger facilities.

Fortunately, the congregation of the Beulah church was made up of very gracious and forgiving people. Forgiveness was given and received in a very Christlike way. They decided to pull together and trust the Lord for the sale of their forty acres of Winterburn property.

Lee and I decided that since the Lord wanted to relocate His church, we would pay the price, whatever that might be, even if it meant that once the project was completed the Lord would lead us to another ministry.

Confronting with Love

While we were waiting for the right land to appear, we still had to carry on our ministry by preaching, working with the elders and managing the church staff. Since there aren't any perfect congregations, people or pastors, much work had to be done to maintain the unity of the Spirit in the bond of peace. "Like an earring of gold or an ornament of fine gold is a wise man's rebuke to a listening ear" (Proverbs 25:12).

It took some courage to face a difficult issue. One night a leading elder drove me home after a late board meeting. We sat in his car parked in my driveway because he had something on his mind to tell me. He warned me that if the board voted a certain way over an issue under discussion, he would resign.

"What do you think about that, pastor?" he asked me.

I replied, "I think you should resign from the board!"

He looked stunned. "What do you mean?"

I explained, "The elders are struggling over a difficult issue. Everyone has the right to debate his view, but when the decision is made the elders must be united. It isn't fair to hold a board hostage to your demands. If you can't be a part of a team, then it is better for everyone involved that you quietly resign. Pray about it tonight and let me know your decision in the morning."

He called the next day to tell me that he would cooperate with the other elders, whatever decision they made. He was true to his word and became a good team player. Most of the time a wise, forthright and loving rebuke in the power of the Spirit of God can correct a person's attitude and behavior and thereby avoid many unpleasant and unnecessary future conflicts.

Managing inexperienced young people isn't an easy job either. I remember one young man's difficult beginning. He became my youth pastor right out of Bible college. At our first pastors' retreat, I outlined my expectations of his ministry. He jumped to his feet and challenged me in front of the other staff, "You are unreasonable. There is no way anyone can do all those things you expect!"

Later, alone with him in my office, I said, "If you can't do the job, I guess I will have to find someone who can."

He broke down in tears. "If I fail so soon after graduation, how will I ever be sure that God called me to the ministry?"

I promised him, "If you will try hard and do your best, I will stand by you, train you and help you succeed."

He became a superstar. Many years later when he left to become the senior pastor of his own church, he and his wife were greatly missed. Today he is a successful pastor.

Searching for Suitable Land

A search committee was formed to find suitable property of sufficient acreage for a large facility to serve 2,000 people in the west end of the city at an affordable price. This wasn't an easy task. On paper, the plan was acceptable by the vast majority of the congregation, but it took a miracle to achieve it. But Jesus said, "I will build my church, and the gates of Hades will not overcome it" (Matthew 16:18).

While searching for the right location, we discovered that a site of four acres was available to purchase from the city. Another church wanted it as well. We began a bidding war, but in the end we lost. We now rejoice because what seemed like a defeat was in reality a blessing from God. The location wasn't the best and it was too small for our congregation's vision.

Keeping to the Task

In the meanwhile I received an unexpected telephone call from the chairman of a pastoral search committee of a large church with a congregation of 2,600 people. He said, "We have looked over forty-five potential candidates and have concluded you are on the top of the list. A few of us want to fly to Edmonton to talk to you." I asked him how he knew of me. He replied, "A couple of our board members attended your church in Omaha. We have listened to a number of your sermon tapes and are convinced you are God's man for our church."

For a short time, I was enticed by the possibility. They already had their new facilities built. I was flattered, but I turned him down. I said, "I can't leave this church until they find land for their relocation, for the sake of their future."

He said, "You must really love those people because you are turning down a great opportunity." (Later, I discovered that they paid their new pastor $100,000 a year!) It wasn't just my love for the congregation that kept me there. I did love them, but I loved my Lord more. Only His call could have made me move before my task was finished.

God Works Behind the Scenes

Our search committee worked diligently but was unable to find land to relocate the church. But what we could not do, God did for us. One day I got an unexpected call from a Jewish businessman in town. "I understand you are looking for land to relocate your church. I have about ten acres that I am willing to sell for a reasonable price. It is close to West Edmonton Mall. Are you interested?"

"Absolutely!" I responded.

After talking awhile, he remarked, "You sound like a Jew."

I replied, "I am Jewish."

"How can you be a pastor of a Christian church and be a Jew at the same time?"

I invited him to lunch to explain it. He warned me not to try to convert him. I assured him, "Only God can do that." We became good friends.

There is an interesting story behind the acquisition of the land. My new Jewish friend and two other developers planned to build high-rise condominiums on the land. The city approved their project, but the market for such a project collapsed during a recession. The developers tried to get the zoning changed, but the city refused all their new proposals. They weren't able to do anything else with their valuable land. One day my new friend had an insightful idea. Maybe, just maybe, a church could influence the city to rezone his land, freeing him to use it for other projects. Later he admitted it was a long shot, which he did not believe could be done. God had planted that idea in his mind.

The city planning commission turned us down flat. We then lobbied every city council member to override the committee's decision. At the beginning of a meeting with two councilwomen, it seemed that our cause was doomed. In my emotional state I even shed a few tears. I pleaded, "You know that Beulah Alliance Church has been a good influence on our city for fifty years. How can I go back to the congregation and tell them that their city leaders won't let them do something good for the city?"

The two members of the council came over to our side. (Watching a grown man weep was something new to them. It turned out to be a rather persuasive argument.) They voted in our favor and, together with other council members, overruled the decision of the planning committee. The planning committee fought hard against us but to no avail.

But all our expertise, planning, strategizing and promoting would have been in vain unless God was in it. While all the glory rightfully belongs to God, the joy of serving Him comes to us.

The third requirement was that our downtown property had to be sold. We had no idea what we could get for it. Our real estate agent told us the market wasn't good for selling an old church. But just when we needed the money, a Greek Orthodox congregation was seeking an older church facility and they paid us $1 million.

Our church was made up of mainly blue-collar workers and government officials. They were without great personal financial resources, but everyone gave what they could. Our congregation sacrificially raised millions of additional dollars for the project without expecting to get their money back from Winterburn in the foreseeable future.

Mission Completed

When my son Peter entered the ministry, I told him never to leave a ministry until God called him to another one. My second exhortation to him was never to leave an assignment incomplete for personal gain. God will reveal the time to depart. This is the advice that I have followed all of my life.

God gave me a full year to enjoy the new facilities and my new study in Edmonton before I went on to accept another challenge. I have learned this much about relocating a church: if the Lord is in it, the project will succeed; however, if the project is motivated by vainglory or by selfish ambition, it will fail.

After ten years as senior pastor, my ministry in Edmonton came to a successful conclusion. God knew me better than I did myself. I am at my best solving problems, facing difficulties, mediating conflicts, overcoming obstacles, leading, organizing and delegating. I have a tendency to delegate myself out of a job. Once a chaotic church gets organized and is moving ahead on the right track, I can get bored. There doesn't seem to be enough challenge left for me. I wonder what to do with myself in a well-run church.

The Edmonton congregation was enjoying their new facilities in a promising area of the city. Every Sunday we were experiencing the rapid growth of the congregation. I knew that God had the right man in mind to succeed me. The obvious blessing of God has been on Pastor Keith Taylor, under whose ministry the church has grown both spiritually and numerically. The attendance of the Beulah Alliance Church is now over 2,200 worshipers every Sunday. I thank my Lord that I have had a share in the success of that great church.

CHAPTER ELEVEN

Leaning on the Holy Spirit

"Not by might nor by power, but by my Spirit," says the LORD Almighty. (Zechariah 4:6)

One of my early assumptions as a senior pastor was that I knew most of what I needed to know about the Christian life. Now that I am in my senior years, I know better. My prayer today is that the Lord will give me the curiosity of a child and the maturity of an adult. I never want to stop asking questions and learning more.

For a long time I thought I knew all about the Holy Spirit and how He works in us and through us, but in reality I was quite ignorant. I resisted allowing the Holy Spirit complete freedom to do whatever He wanted because I was afraid of losing control. I feared fanaticism. My fear hindered me from some wonderful blessings. The most surprising truth that I have discovered about the Holy Spirit is His longsuffering with us. This is evident in the gracious work He has done through my ministries.

Satan does all he can to frighten us away from trusting God's Spirit in order to deny us spiritual power. Some years ago, when I was speaking at a church in Maine, a man drove 100 miles to tell me his story. He went to a retreat that emphasized the Spirit-filled life. After checking into the conference and while unpacking his suitcase, he heard a voice say, "Let me live my life in you." Six months later he woke up in a mental hospital with no memory of what had happened to put him there.

Later he was told what happened to him at the retreat. He ran out of the room raving incoherently at the top of his voice. Jumping into his car, he drove erratically on the wrong side of a superhighway. The state police finally caught up to him, arrested him and committed him to the mental institution. A psychiatrist informed his wife that her husband was incurably insane. Six months later his sanity returned. He warned me to be careful.

What I did not know at the time was that Satan was attempting to frighten me away from depending on the Holy Spirit. Obviously that man had encountered a false spirit who took over his mind.

The Bible tells us in Second Timothy 1:7: "For God has not given us a spirit of fear, but of power and of love and of a sound mind" (NKJV). And, "The Lord is the Spirit, and where the Spirit of the Lord is, there is freedom" (2 Corinthians 3:17).

In Galatians 5:22-23, the Bible also informs us that the fruit of the Spirit is self-control. The Spirit of God produces freedom, a sound mind and self-control within us.

As a teenaged Christian, I acquired some strange misconceptions about the Spirit-filled life. I heard preachers declare, "Jesus wants to live His life through us. Our hands are His only hands, our feet are the only feet, and our mouths are the only mouth. Think of yourself as an empty shell and let Him take over."

Taking that theology literally led me to pray foolishly, "Lord, I have a proposal for You: take over my consciousness for the next ten years. Live Your life in me. Take me through

The absurdity of that request wasn't obvious to me at the time. Now I understand better. What if the Lord had taken over my mind at the age of fourteen and then woke me up years later to give me back control of my life? I would still be an immature teenager intellectually and socially. The difficulties we face over the years aren't easy but they are necessary to develop maturity and competence.

The Lord doesn't want to usurp our minds and suppress our personalities. God seeks to develop us into mature sons and daughters, not robots. Demons desire to take over the control of the human mind and body to live out their selfish existence; that is not God's way. The Spirit of the Lord brings liberation and freedom, not bondage.

How can we be sure that we are dealing with the true Spirit of God and not a deceptive spirit? Very easily! We already know the Holy Spirit if we are God's children. All true Christians have the indwelling of the Holy Spirit.

The Bible tells us, "Repent and be baptized, every one of you, in the name of Jesus Christ for the forgiveness of your sins. And you will receive the gift of the Holy Spirit. The promise is for you and your children and for all who are far off—for all whom the Lord our God will call" (Acts 2:38-39).

I cannot answer for anyone else's experience, only my own. I know the Holy Spirit. He was the One who revealed Jesus to me and gave me the assurance of the forgiveness of all my sins. He is the One who is leading me into a meaningful and balanced life.

Trusting the Holy Spirit

I feared that if I opened up my church to spiritual demonstrations, demons would creep in and cause havoc. I imagined some might bark like dogs, climb trees like monkeys and jabber with strange noises. By fearing the false, I limited the true work of God's Spirit. My fears were ungrounded because the Holy Spirit does not promote chaos; He is the Author of order and unity.

Two events freed me from my fears of fanaticism and losing control over my congregation. First, my confidence in Dr. Peter Wagner, my mentor in church growth, freed me from the fear of allowing the Holy Spirit to do what He desired within the church. One day Peter had shared his liberating experience with the Holy Spirit. After a class, I chided him, "You have a great deal of credibility around the world, which places a lot of responsibility on your shoulders. You must be careful never to mislead the people who trust you. Now tell me, do you really believe in what you are teaching about the Holy Spirit?" I looked straight into his eyes to see if there were any doubts of his position. Without a blink, he replied, "Yes I do!" With that affirmative answer, I began to give his ideas some serious consideration.

The second event that freed me to trust the Spirit of God for His miraculous interventions came out of my own frustrations with powerlessness. When people came to me with their deep-seated problems, I referred them to some other professional expert. I sent them away with a brief prayer and a handshake. It dawned on me that I wasn't helping people. One day I prayed a prayer of desperation. A new and exciting ministry began out of my frustration of seeing so many defeated Christians in the church. I became willing to take a new look at the work of the Holy Spirit.

I should have known better since I had studied at two Alliance schools and a Wesleyan Methodist college where the work of the Holy Spirit and sanctification were taught and emphasized. Yet I remained confused about Him and was unable to articulate the theology of the Holy Spirit. The schools were not at fault; I just wasn't ready to let go of my fears. I confess that I was afraid of becoming labeled as an extremist and a fanatic by other Christians. Surprisingly, I discovered that A.B. Simpson, the founder of The Christian and Missionary Alliance, the famous evangelist, D.L. Moody and the world renowned Bible teacher, R.A. Torrey, all preached the necessity of the filling of the Holy Spirit subsequent to conversion. They insisted that the second work of grace was essential for victorious living.

Controversies over theological terms such as "the baptism of the Holy Spirit," "the filling of the Holy Spirit" and "the second work of grace" have torn many congregations apart. Even devout Christian families have been divided over these theological terms.

Some object to the term "a second work of grace" on the grounds that it minimizes all the other works of God's grace. Without a doubt, there are many more works of God's grace than just two. Every answer to a prayer is a work of God's grace. However, most Christians agree that there is another step to take after conversion, even though they argue over terms. Some call the second step "consecration" while others call it "sanctification." One group focuses on the responsibility of a Christian to consecrate himself to God after his conversion according to Romans 12:1: "Therefore, I urge you, brothers, in view of God's mercy, to offer your bodies as living sacrifices, holy and pleasing to God—this is your spiritual act of worship."

The others focus on what God does within a person at the time of his consecration. Their focus is on Romans 12:2: "Do not conform any longer to the pattern of this world, but be transformed by the renewing of your mind. Then you will be able to test and approve what God's will is—his good, pleasing and perfect will."

The phrase "renewing of your mind" is in the passive voice. Connected with our consecration is the inner working of the Spirit, transforming and renewing our minds, which enables us to know and live out His good, pleasing and perfect will for our lives.

The filling of the Holy Spirit begins a deeper process of an inner transformation of the heart and mind of a Christian. We must be progressively changed from within. Only then will our thinking and behavior improve. The Bible explains the workings of God within us: "May . . . God . . . through . . . our Lord Jesus, that great Shepherd of the sheep, equip you with everything good for doing his will, and may he work in us what is pleasing to him, through Jesus Christ, to whom be glory for ever and ever. Amen" (Hebrews 13:20-21).

Consecration is what we do and sanctification is what God does for us. A person may consecrate himself a thousand times over and shed a million tears of repentance and yet be no better off unless God grants to him sanctifying grace.

When my wife and I arrived in Israel in 1995 for a missionary opportunity, a missionary met us at the airport in Tel Aviv. On our way to Jerusalem, he asked me, "Do you remember the deeper life conference you held at Toccoa Falls College in 1978? I was a long-haired student on probation then. Even as a Christian, I struggled with my old life. You were preaching on Romans 6. I went to the altar defeated in my spirit, but I returned to my seat a victorious Christian." Think of it! In a moment, God's grace set him completely free from destructive behavior.

I am convinced of the absolute necessity of cooperating with God in order to obtain His gifts of grace. Our Lord Jesus has provided eternal life as a gift, but we are required to accept it by an act of our will. What is true for salvation is also true for sanctification. Furthermore, each day we must decide to walk in the Spirit and not in the flesh. God does not force Himself or His gifts on anyone, but once we submit to His authority willingly, He does it all for us.

The Bible tells us, "May God himself, the God of peace, sanctify you through and through. May your whole spirit, soul and body be kept blameless at the coming of our Lord Jesus Christ. The one who calls you is faithful and he will do it" (1 Thessalonians 5:23-24).

I now have a better understanding of the biblical doctrine of the Holy Spirit and how our experience fits into it. While every true believer has the indwelling presence of the Holy Spirit, not every Christian adequately cooperates with Him. I heard an illustration of this idea in the story of a man who invited his elderly mother to come and live in his house with a few "reasonable" stipulations.

"Mother," he said, "we want you to live with us, but keep in mind that we have active lives of our own. We have fixed up a one-bedroom apartment next to our large furnace room in the basement. You have your own private entrance to come and go as you wish, but please stay there unless we invite you to come upstairs." Rarely was the mother ever invited to be with the family.

At the dinner table one evening, his four-year-old daughter cheerfully said, "Daddy, when you are old, you can come and live in my basement." The father got the picture of the bad example he was setting down for his children. He realized that it might affect his own future. He quickly invited his mother out of the basement to live upstairs as a part of the family.

Whether the illustration is of a true experience or not isn't important, because the application is valid. We must allow the Holy Spirit to have complete access to all areas of our lives. The Holy Spirit resides in all true Christians. The Bible tells us, "[God] set his seal of ownership on us, and put his Spirit in our hearts as a deposit, guaranteeing what is to come" (2 Corinthians 1:22).

Unfortunately some of us keep Him in the basements of our lives. We don't receive Him very well. We do not cooperate with Him. If we are to experience His fullness, we need to turn all the keys of our lives over to Him. The relevant question for a true Christian is not how can we obtain the Holy Spirit, but how should we behave toward Him? He is more than a guest; the Spirit is the very Source of our life in Christ. Let us acknowledge His authority and follow His counsel.

Being a Channel for the Holy Spirit

In John 7:38-39, Jesus said, " 'Whoever believes in me, as the Scripture has said, streams of living water will flow from within him.' By this he meant the Spirit, whom those who believed in him were later to receive." While our Lord Jesus is the only Source of the Holy Spirit, He intends us to be the channels of His Spirit to the world. Reflecting on my own genuine experience with the filling and fellowship of the Holy Spirit, I desired to connect others with Him, so I prayed, "Lord, I am not satisfied in sending people away as defeated as they came seeking for You. You have provided power for Your children to live holy and useful lives. Forgive me for ignoring the message of the filling of the Holy Spirit. How can I duplicate the filling of the Spirit in the lives of others?"

A phrase from Hebrews 6:1-2 seized my attention: "The doctrine . . . of laying on of hands" (KJV). That phrase stuck in my mind. I had felt for many years that "laying on of hands" while praying for someone was on the edge of fanaticism. I never considered such an activity as authentic. No one ever laid his hands on me the day I was filled with the Spirit. However, since I was desperate to see God work, I was willing to try this possibility. I realize that the circumstances around spiritual experiences vary from person to person. Spiritual experiences aren't always replicated in the same way since God works uniquely with each person. While I still don't fully understand the significance of the "laying on of hands," I have seen its value in providing an occasion for a divine encounter between the Spirit and a true seeker.

The early Church practiced the "laying on of hands" for various purposes: to heal the sick, to set someone apart for the ministry, to convey a blessing from God and to impart the filling of the Spirit. Since I was convinced of the necessity of the filling of the Spirit for every Christian, I was willing to try anything.

I sought the counsel and cooperation of my elders. I inquired about their reaction to laying my hands on people who were seeking for God in the privacy of my office. They were surprised that I would even ask for their permission—they were far ahead of me. An elder spoke up: "Pastor, we trust you to do God's will." I assured them that I was pragmatic and would cease the practice if God didn't bless it.

The first one to see me after the approval of the elders was a woman who sat on the other side of my desk with despair written on her face. After a brief period of uneasy silence, she came right to the point: "Pastor, I hate God." I asked her if anyone else knew about it. "No," she replied. "No one—not my husband, nor my children, nor my Christian friends."

Her honesty unnerved me. She had caught me off-guard. I spoke a few encouraging words to cheer her up, but I wasn't ready to counsel her right then. I then asked for some time to think and pray over her problem. Before she left, she gave me permission to lay my hands on her head and pray for her. She promised to return at the same time a week later. She left my office just as depressed as she had come in. She was my first test case and it didn't appear to be working.

The next week she returned for her appointment. "Pastor," she began, "at the Sunday service, God opened my eyes to see myself. I understand now that it's not God's fault that I hate Him, but my own."

That was the breakthrough I had hoped for. I gave her an exercise to complete. I asked her to write down everything God had shown her about herself, including all her wrong attitudes and behavior. I told her, "After you complete your list, confess everything to God, then tear up the list into tiny pieces. When you are finished dealing with God, open the door to let me know you are ready for me to return."

All I did was place my hands on her head again and pray a simple prayer. No conversation or counseling went on between us. I then went behind my desk and sat down. I waited for her to get up and leave. She just sat there motionless and silent for what seemed a long time.

"Is there anything else you want to say? Is anything wrong?" I asked her.

She replied, "I can't move."

I was alarmed and concerned until she explained what was happening to her. "The love of God is filling my soul with waves of joy," she told me.

"Stay seated until God completes His work in you," I told her. As I watched her unhappy expression transfigure into a look of ecstasy, I silently prayed, *Lord, why not me?* But this was God's special experience for her alone. Later she became an effective prayer counselor for others who were struggling with their relationship with God.

After that experience, I became courageous about laying hands on people who wanted to be filled with the Holy Spirit. Canadian Bible College in Regina invited me to speak on the Holy Spirit. My sermon topic was announced to the students prior to my coming: "Don't Be Afraid of the Holy Spirit." After my message, I invited interested students to stay behind so I could lay my hands on them and pray that Jesus would fill them with His Holy Spirit. I expected two or three to remain. Surprisingly, few left the chapel. Most of the student body just sat there waiting for me to pray for them. Since no one was prepared to assist me, it took about an hour to finish.

A few years later, Dr. Arnold Cook, the past president of the Canadian Alliance, wrote me an encouraging letter stating that two students he interviewed for overseas ministries testified of being filled with the Holy Spirit when I prayed for them at that chapel.

As I am maturing in my understanding of the ministry of the Spirit, I realize the attention should not be on the ritual of laying on of hands, nor should it be on the one who prays for the seeker, but only on our Lord Jesus. He alone is the Source of the Holy Spirit. One of the values of the "laying on of hands" is that it provides an occasion, an opportunity, for a divine encounter and a consecrated moment for a seeker after God. The prophet Jeremiah wrote, " 'Then you will call upon me and come and pray to me, and I will listen to you. You will seek me and find me when you seek me with all your heart. I will be found by you,' declares the LORD" (Jeremiah 29:12-14).

Steps to Be Filled with the Spirit

There are three steps to take in order to be filled with the Holy Spirit. I say this generally and not dogmatically, because God may work in new and unique ways to fill His individual children with the Holy Spirit.

First, we must invite God's Spirit to search our hearts. Trying to understand ourselves can lead us to a dead end. Our ego defense mechanisms will misdirect us into denial, self-justification and rationalization. Or our pride may lead us to false guilt and self-condemnation, which refuses to accept God's gracious forgiveness. Only the Holy Spirit can search our hearts and reveal the truth to us.

Secondly, we must confess the sins God shows us. We will experience all kinds of unpleasant emotions at first, such as surprise, shame, shock, humiliation, fear, regret and sincere sorrow. Such godly sorrow leads to repentance that results in joy. The Bible tells us the value of this pain in Second Corinthians 7:9: "Your sorrow led you to repentance. For you became sorrowful as God intended and so were not harmed in any way." This may be a painful process but it prepares us to receive the Spirit of God in His fullness.

Thirdly, we must ask the Lord Jesus to fill us with the Holy Spirit. Only when we acknowledge Jesus as our Lord and submit completely to His authority are we ready to experience the filling of the Spirit. There is generally a crisis aspect to enter into a sanctified life, but there is also a subsequent progressive phase of spiritual growth, which is a daily walk with God.

"But if we walk in the light, as he is in the light, we have fellowship with one another, and the blood of Jesus, his Son, purifies us from all sin" (1 John 1:7). The seeker's motivation is the main issue with God. If a person is seeking only for spiritual power to have influence over other people, for personal gain or pursuing personal goodness to obtain the admiration of others, he is bound to be disappointed.

Rediscovering the Healing Ministry

While in Edmonton, I became more receptive to a healing ministry. Only after accepting my place as a servant of God did I begin to receive insights into divine healing. I learned that God may respond to our prayers for healing in one of three ways.

God may heal completely and instantaneously

I saw this while I was representing the Jewish mission years before. I was invited to speak at a Mennonite church. After the service, I noticed a girl about six years old with an unusually beautiful rosy complexion. She was jumping and running around with her playmates. "That is one healthy-looking girl," I remarked.

An elderly lady who introduced herself as the girl's grandmother overheard me. "You would not have said that a few months ago," she said. "My granddaughter was dying of an incurable liver disease. Her doctor told us that she would be dead by morning. An all-night prayer meeting was called to pray for her. After the prayer meeting, we returned home. As we got into the house, we heard the phone ringing. The little girl's mother picked up the phone and heard the nurse at the hospital tell her to come quickly. The doctor wanted to see her. Thinking her daughter had died, she fainted.

"We rushed to the hospital, expecting the worst. The doctor was in the hallway outside the little girl's room, leaning against the wall and shaking his head in bewilderment. 'I don't understand it,' he said. 'Last night I left the girl in a coma. Her complexion was a sickly yellow. Her stomach was as hard as a rock. She was comatose and dying. This morning, I came in to see her and her complexion was beautiful. She was alert and hungry. She has been eating without any problem.' "

It was a miracle. Certainly the combined prayers of His people moved God to grant health to that sick little girl. I will always remember that miracle of God's grace.

Sometimes God doesn't answer our prayer for healing the first time we pray. A man came to me with a physical need. For twenty-one years he had suffered with chronic fatigue syndrome. It had gotten so oppressive that he was ready to sell his business. I encouraged him to come and be anointed and prayed for by the elders. Later, when I discovered that God had not healed him, I invited him to come and be prayed for again. Reluctantly he agreed, but God still did not heal him. A third time I invited him to come for prayer. It took a while before he came. This time, God healed him.

I gave this example at an Alliance Council. Two years later, at another Council, a pastor told me that he had been anointed and prayed for twice without any success. He concluded that God wasn't going to heal him of his chronic fatigue syndrome, and he was preparing to leave the ministry. When he heard my message, he decided to be prayed for again. This time God healed him completely. Persistent prayer pleases God.

God may heal in collaboration with the medical profession

Thank God for medical advances such as insulin, antidepressants, high blood pressure medication, antibiotics, a host of other medicines and lifesaving surgical procedures!

If a diabetic tells me, "Pray for my healing, and I will promise not to take insulin anymore!" I refuse to do it. When God heals, doctors will confirm it.

We all need a physician at times. The wife of a pastor friend began behaving very strangely. She often fell into an emotional slump and reacted by insulting the people of the congregation. Nothing helped her overcome her bizarre behavior. Counseling and even exorcism did not work for her. I suggested antidepressants.

"No way!" declared her pastor husband. "This is a spiritual problem." He concluded that either she had not confessed some sins in her life or she was under a demonic attack. Strange how we are so ready to spiritualize all our problems.

Finally, out of desperation, the pastor's wife accepted the advice of her Christian physician and went on antidepressants. Her quick and complete recovery was amazing. The pastor's wife became her former sweet self again.

God may decide to heal a person's spirit

While the Lord does not always heal His children physically, He will always grant them strength and grace. Sometimes our need is for sanctifying grace. During a period of time that it seemed everyone who came for healing was healed, a young woman came forward in her wheelchair for prayer. She requested healing from muscular dystrophy. The next Sunday

I saw her still in her wheelchair. I sympathetically said to her, "I am sorry that the Lord did not heal you."

"Don't be," she replied with a radiant face. "God did something better for me. For years I hated my family for cheating me out of my inheritance. When you prayed for me, all my bitterness evaporated and in its place I was filled with God's forgiving love for my family." God's grace had healed her heart.

Rather than healing a terminal illness, God may give dying grace. After all, we will all eventually die. God may say, "Not this time, my child. It is time to come home!" Ever since I started in the ministry, I have ministered to the terminally ill. Somehow I felt responsible for their healing. I earnestly prayed for their healing and felt like a failure when they died. I finally came to a realization that there is a time for healing and a time for dying. Everyone has to depart from this life. Giving false hope to one facing death is a lost opportunity to prepare them for eternity. The greatest joy I began to experience was to share the reality of heaven with God's children.

Working with terminally ill patients forced me to deal with my own mortality. Some time ago, I said to the Lord, "The present world seems so real, and heaven seems so far away and unreal to me. Allow me to sense heaven before I die." I prayed without expecting anything special to happen, but I have discovered that our heavenly Father takes our requests seriously. When I least expected it to take place, it happened. I was relaxing and thinking about something else when suddenly heaven's atmosphere of love and glory began filling my room. Its reality progressively intensified. Heaven became so real to me that I was afraid of being swept away into heaven before my time.

I did not want to leave behind a young widow with four small children, so I cried out, "Lord, heaven is real enough for me." Foolishly I feared that God would end my earthly life before it was His time for me to go. Hebrews 12:22-24 comforted me that in His good time I would experience this joy again.

> But you have come to Mount Zion, to the heavenly Jerusalem, the city of the living God. You have come to thousands upon thousands of angels in joyful assembly, to the church of the firstborn, whose names are written in heaven. You have come to God, the judge of all men, to the spirits of righteous men made perfect, to Jesus the mediator of a new covenant.

A retired holiness preacher, a treasured friend, had a recurrence of a previous cancer. The prognosis wasn't good. His physicians gave him just a few months to live. He shared with me that fifteen years earlier he had been given up to die from cancer. He had petitioned the Lord to add fifteen years to his life. To the amazement of his physicians, the cancer went into remission. Now, after all that time, the cancer had returned with a vengeance. He didn't understand why God wouldn't heal him again. He went into a deep depression. In his darkest moments, he questioned his very salvation. I explained, "No wonder you are so depressed with all the strong medication in you, along with a malicious cancer breaking down your body. Now is the time to go by faith, not by feelings." I wanted him to focus his attention on heaven, so I read some of the eternal promises of God from Scripture:

> Now we know that if the earthly tent we live in is destroyed, we have a building from God, an eternal house in heaven, not built by human hands. . . . Now it is God who has made us for this very purpose and has given us the Spirit as a deposit, guaranteeing what is to come.

> Therefore we are always confident and know that as long as we are at home in the body we are away from the Lord. We live by faith, not by sight. We are confident, I say, and would prefer to be away from the body and at home with the Lord. So we make it our goal to please him, whether we are at home in the body or away from it. (2 Corinthians 5:1-9)

I then laid hands on him and prayed that our Lord would grant him dying grace. Later, his wife informed me that her husband never doubted his salvation again, but died in peace, leaving behind a witness of God's grace for his family and friends.

People have asked me if I understand why God heals some people, but not all who prayed for it. No, I don't! God is sovereign and free to do whatever He wishes. I have seen useful people die and troublemakers healed. I knew people with strong faith who died, and others with no apparent faith who were healed.

Some assume that since God doesn't always heal everyone, they won't pray for healing. Isn't it wiser to conclude that since God is still healing some people, we shouldn't hesitate to ask for it?

I do not possess a gift of healing. I have prayed for people who were wondrously healed, some who were partially healed and others who were not healed. I haven't found a formula in the Bible that guarantees healing every time, but I have learned something about our Lord Jesus. A sincere prayer of faith can influence Him to heal us. Jesus compassionately understands our pain because He experienced all kinds of pain. The pain of poverty, of social rejection, of misunderstanding by those He loved, of betrayal by a close friend, of rejection by His own people, of suffering injustice, of physical pain and of death itself.

> For we do not have a high priest who cannot sympathize with our weaknesses, but one who has been tempted in all things as we are, yet without sin. Let us therefore draw near with confidence to the throne of grace, that we may receive mercy and find grace to help in time of need. (Hebrews 4:15-16, NASB)

CHAPTER TWELVE

Accepting a Transitional Ministry

Then I heard the voice of the Lord saying, "Whom shall I send? And who will go for us?" And I said, "Here am I. Send me!" (Isaiah 6:8)

Reminiscing over my past ministries of forty-five years, I have come to realize that God has called me to be His troubleshooter. As a new Christian, I had a teenage desire to be an important member of God's team. I imagined God saying, "Who can we get to do that difficult job that no one else wants? I know I can depend on Albert to do it." Seeing the imaginations of my heart, God may have decided to satisfy my desire by fulfilling His promise in Psalm 37:4-5: "Delight yourself in the LORD and he will give you the desires of your heart. Commit your way to the LORD; trust in him and he will do this."

My personality requires tackling tough situations even though it may create anxiety for others and myself. My faith needs stretching almost to the breaking point to keep my life interesting and challenged.

The best time to leave a church is when everything is going well. So with the freedom of the Spirit, I accepted an invitation for an interview from the pastoral search committee of the Sevenoaks Alliance Church in Abbotsford, British Columbia. I was not absolutely certain why the committee asked me to come for an interview in light of the fact that I was sixty-two years old. I explained to the search committee that because of my age, I could not commit myself to a long-term position. The men recognized that a transitional pastor was their greatest need at the time; consequently, they asked me to be their candidate. After my interview and invitation to candidate, I decided not to follow through without my wife's agreement since I have come to depend on Lee's wisdom and good judgment over the years. She did not want me to meet with the committee because she was happy and satisfied in Edmonton with her friends. I kept putting my candidating date off. Finally, I made a bargain with Lee. "Look, honey," I said, "I have to go and see if this is God's will for us. Come along with me. I promise not to accept the opportunity unless you are for it."

So Lee came along, dragging her feet all the way to British Columbia. Lee determined not to be influenced by anyone, including me. On the Sunday morning when I was to candidate officially, Lee predicted with a smile that we were going to be called by the church. I warned her not to get too enthusiastic and become disappointed. Nothing that I said could discourage her. During the interview with the elders, Lee did a better job candidating for the position than I did. I asked her what had changed her attitude. She told me that that very morning during her devotions, God had revealed that He wanted us to serve the Sevenoaks Alliance Church. She would never refuse God.

After the morning service the elders gave me the call to be their pastor. The chairman wanted to discuss my salary. I had heard from a reliable source that although it was the largest Alliance church in Canada, its staff wasn't paid the best salary. I assured the elders that I have never made my salary the condition for my ministry, but I shared with them what the Edmonton church paid me. There was a period of dead silence. I heard a few elders groan under their breath. One elder objected, "If we pay you that much, we will have to raise the salaries of all the staff."

I replied, "Good idea! We trust God for buildings and missions; we can also trust God to pay His servants a livable salary."

Another elder asked me, "Just how much can you get by on?"

I replied, "I am not going to answer that question, but let me ask you a question. How much do you think I am worth? You are asking me to do a big and complex job. Keep in mind it is my responsibility to raise the money needed for the budget."

I not only got a good salary, but the staff also got raises. God provided, and we finished every year with a surplus. In addition, the church eliminated $1 million from their debt during my three years of service.

When I arrived in January of 1991, I attempted to understand the church's situation. I discovered that in 1987, the Sevenoaks Alliance Church had an average attendance of 2,000 worshipers every Sunday. Three years later, the yearly attendance dropped to under 1,500. There were some very good reasons for the decline. Sevenoaks had planted three daughter churches in the area. They gave about 300 people to the new congregations. Four of their pastors had left for other ministries. They had all resigned within months of each other, leaving behind a grieving congregation.

Restoring such a church to effectiveness isn't easy. The task was complicated by the diversity of the congregation. The Sevenoaks membership came from thirty-nine different denominational traditions as well as from a mixture of ethnic backgrounds. In addition, it was an intergenerational congregation. Some wanted traditional hymns; others, contemporary worship music. Some expected exegetical expository sermons that were deeply rooted in theological concepts, while others wanted simple biblical messages full of inspiring stories that were applicable to life situations. Some expected their new senior pastor to be gentle, soft-spoken and sweet to everybody, a pastor like they had once known and loved. Others wanted a prophet, while others thought the church needed an evangelist. All in all the church was made up of reasonable people. Everyone had his own reasonable expectations of the pastor, but multitudes of reasonable expectations combined are unattainable.

The Sevenoaks Alliance Church had many valuable assets that contributed to their prominence in Canada. The congregation was composed mainly of good-hearted and generous people. There was a staff of ten pastors covering a variety of ministries from children to senior citizens. A supportive board of godly elders encouraged me. The congregation had a strong missionary vision along with a desire to evangelize their community. I could not ask for a better opportunity.

When a new pastor arrives at a church, the congregation and the church board welcome him with complete confidence in his ability to fulfill their expectations. As time progresses, a pastor makes recommendations. If his proposals succeed his leadership is enhanced, but if they fail his credibility decreases. There is a level of disappointment that will make it impossible for a failing pastor to recover his leadership of the church. These were the things that I needed to take into consideration as I began my work at Sevenoaks.

Seeking Guidance from the Elders

My first objective was to get to know my elders. I wanted to know their concerns for the church and their expectations of me. A surprise was in store for me. At my first meeting with the elders, my agenda was composed of just a few questions. I asked them, "Are you expecting me to be a leader or a chaplain?" Every elder expressed his view, and without exception they wanted me to be the leader. They gave me a job profile that included not only administrating the church but also doing most of the preaching. That was a radical shift from the role of their former senior pastor who was required only to administrate the church.

Secondly, I asked them, "What are your concerns?" Every elder expressed concerns about the effectiveness of various ministries. My favorable impression of the condition of the church prior to accepting the call was fading fast. The organization wasn't working as smoothly as I had been led to believe. They all agreed that major improvements were needed.

Thirdly, I asked them, "What do you expect me to do about your concerns?"

"Make major changes," was their reply to a man. I knew changes would create stress and conflicts, especially in an older congregation. Mark Twain once said, "The only person who likes change is a wet baby." I sat traumatized. My hope for an easy assignment in my old age had evaporated into thin air. I then asked the board a question that only time could answer. "Where will you be when the complaining begins?"

On behalf of the whole board, one elder said, "Pastor, we will be right there behind you all the way!" I thought to myself, *How far behind will they be when the complaining begins?* Lay leaders can soon lose their courage in the midst of conflicts. One elder said, "Pastor, we want you to make changes, but don't hurt anyone doing it." Such directions are like saying to a surgeon, "My mother is sick and I know she must have an operation to recover her health, but you can do it only if it doesn't hurt." The process of even beneficial change is painful.

Because I understood the potential of conflicts in such a transition, I decided that my first objective was to train the elders in church dynamics and conflict management as quickly as possible. I wanted to prepare them for the inevitable discord. We met every week during the Sunday school hour.

Building the Team

My second objective was to get to know my staff before any plan of action could be formulated. Understandably, they expected me to fit into their old routine and their way of doing things. The staff wasn't prepared for an aggressive Jewish pastor who liked being a change agent. The younger members of the staff got along well with me. I loved being their mentor and they appreciated learning from me. We also had a lot of fun together and developed long-term friendships.

It is natural that when a new senior pastor arrives, some staff members decide to leave. Some people found it hard to accept the resignation of a staff member they loved and respected and just weren't ready for a new senior pastor's arrival. The congregation had already suffered the loss of four significant pastors before I came on the scene. For all the congregation knew, I was autocratically taking over their church, getting rid of some of their pastors and making unnecessary changes just to suit my fancy. They were not informed of the mandate given to me by the elders.

Managing a large staff is difficult for an average congregation to understand. Most Christians grow up in small or medium-size churches, where their sole pastor served as a chaplain, not as the leader. There was no other staff to manage. Their pastor did all the work of the ministry. He preached at every service and visited all the members at least twice a year, while the elders administrated the business affairs of the church. All that is reversed in a larger church. The pastor is the leader and administrator of a complex church while the people are equipped to do the work of the ministry.

The differences between a small church and a large church can be illustrated by a comparison between a sailboat with a few friends having fun crossing a lake and an aircraft carrier with a captain and a crew of thousands going into battle. In addition to his leadership skills, the senior pastor must manage a pastoral team or delegate that task to an executive pastor, who in turn must mobilize the professional staff to equip the laity to do the work of the ministry.

We kept most of the staff and added other well-trained pastors who were gifted for specialized ministries. We added five new specialists to the staff. Dr. Clyde Glass was the pastor of leadership development and mobilization of lay pastors. They were trained to create and care for small groups. David Phillips, the minister of counseling and support groups, organized and supervised a lay and professional Christian counseling center, various support groups and marriage retreats. Mrs. Rita Lahaven brought many good innovations to the children's ministries. Pastor Steve Reibsome, the minister of music, added contemporary worship music to the services. Mr. Art Sauder, the church administrator, used his business skills to supervise the secretarial and custodial staff as well as administrating the business of the church.

Some consider me stubborn, but I think of myself as a persevering person who is steadfast in purpose. When I believe I am on an assignment from God and see clearly what must be done, I don't easily let go of the goal in mind. I persisted in my mandate to bring about the necessary changes for the future good of the church. In just three years, I added forty-three innovations to the church and a number of new ministries as well. The most exciting for me was the open-altar ministry.

The Open Prayer Altar

I sensed there was an important element missing from the church services. I always tried my best to arrange upbeat, inspirational music, a positive sermon, a relevant closing hymn and an inspiring benediction, but I did not program any time for the Holy Spirit to deal with individuals. After the benediction, the congregation quickly became distracted, chatting with friends, gathering their children and rushing out to dinner.

I became aware of excellent evangelical ministers who preach Spirit-inspired, heart-searching and powerful, motivational messages without results. They are like fishermen who throw their nets out into the ocean but neglect to pull it back in with the fish.

When Jesus called His disciples, He told them, " 'Come, follow me . . . and I will make you fishers of men.' At once they left their nets and followed him" (Mark 1:17-18).

For many years in the past, I resisted inviting people to come to the altar. I justified my reluctance with the idea that it wasn't relevant in our contemporary culture. Secretly I feared giving an altar call because of my pride. What if the congregation was unresponsive and no one came to the altar during the invitation? I visualized myself standing awkwardly by an empty altar, looking foolish. The last thing I wanted was to experience the humiliation of failure.

The strategy of the open prayer altar came out of my desire to help people connect with God. I knew there were many hurting people who sat in the congregation week after week not knowing how to get in touch with God. It was obvious to me that many people were leaving church Sunday after Sunday still carrying all their burdens and guilt. That realization sent me on a quest to find a strategy that could bring people and God together. I prayed for guidance: "Lord Jesus, many people come to church every week with a smile on their faces but with tears in their hearts. They are seeking Your help. Sending them away disappointed doesn't help them or bring glory to You. What can I do to link them up with You?"

An idea came to my mind. What about operating an open prayer altar, where a seeker did not have to fear unjust criticism from others? It would not be exclusively for unbelievers and backsliders. Anyone, for any reason, could come and pray. They may come to thank God for a special blessing, to intercede for a friend, to seek healing, to confess a sin, for a divine intervention in a domestic conflict or for any other reason. The open altar has an all-encompassing purpose, unlike the old mourner's bench that invited only sinners to repentance. The open altar invitation isn't necessarily tied to the theme of the sermon, which may exclude many from coming to the altar.

An invitation to the open prayer altar gives the Holy Spirit significant time in the service to deal personally with individuals. It provides people with an opportunity to respond immediately to the prompting of the Spirit before the service is dismissed. A valid transaction with God takes only a few minutes. Unless there is an appropriate opportunity to respond to Him, a divine encounter may be missed forever. A person is mostly likely to respond to God during a serious crisis or a moment of unusual tenderness. The Bible exhorts us, "Today, if you hear his voice, do not harden your hearts" (Hebrews 4:7).

A Trial Run

Out of my frustration of seeing good people leave the church with their problems unresolved, I decided to try my idea. If nothing happened, I would look for another approach. The test was a success. An elderly couple was the first to come forward at the invitation. They told me about an angry fight they had had with their daughter fifteen years before. She stormed out of the house and disappeared from sight. They had searched for her without success and weren't sure if she was alive or dead. Her father told me, "We are getting older and our fear is increasing that we will die before we can become reconciled with her."

I explicitly prayed, "Lord, wherever their daughter might be right now, near or far away, put it into her heart to call her parents before this week is over."

Ordinarily, it isn't a good idea to set time limits on God. He works in His own way and time. We can't rush the Lord to do our bidding. Such a specific prayer can raise false expectations in anxious people that might end in deep disappointment.

The Lord was merciful in accepting and answering our prayer. Four days later, early in the morning, their phone rang and woke them out of a sound sleep. To their surprise it was their daughter calling them. Later that month, they met together and with many tears became a unified family again.

I used to be critical of evangelists singing all four verses of an invitation hymn. I now understand that the Spirit needs time to struggle with some people. Generally people do not come to church thinking God is going to speak to them that very day.

They aren't prepared to respond. Every time the Spirit confronts a person, a battle goes on for an eternal soul. The devil doesn't want to lose control over souls.

It takes humility to walk down a long aisle to kneel at the prayer altar before the entire congregation. Pride is the greatest hindrance to prayer. Pride is self-sufficient and self-glorifying. Pride doesn't admit a need, nor does it want to be indebted to anyone, especially to God. The Bible warns the proud in First Peter 5:5-7: " 'God opposes the proud but gives grace to the humble.' Humble yourselves, therefore, under God's mighty hand, that he may lift you up in due time. Cast all your anxiety on him because he cares for you."

Many people who found answers to their prayers at the altar have asked me to explain a mystery: "How is it that I have privately prayed about my need for years, but nothing happened? Then, when I came to the altar and prayed about that same problem—God granted my request soon after. How do you explain that, pastor?"

I can't explain every mystery, but I have discovered that there is something special about what the Lord does in the assembly of His people. When we meet together in the congregation, we meet with Jesus. The Bible tells us in Hebrews 2:11-12: "Jesus is not ashamed to call them brothers. He says, 'I will declare your name to my brothers; in the presence of the congregation I will sing your praises.' "

Many evangelical churches are losing their appreciation for the reality of the supernatural presence of Jesus in every service. That may be the reason so many churches have canceled their evening service. God's people must understand that when the congregation gathers, Christ's presence and power are available in a special way. The older I get, the more I realize the importance of being an active part of a church family. Each of us are only a small part of that body. Even as an ear needs an eye and a foot needs an arm to function adequately, so we are in need of one another to fully experience the life of Christ.

We can't make it spiritually on our own. Obviously, God does answer prayers made in the secret of one's own home, but He especially loves to answer public prayer in order to encourage others to trust Him to help in difficult times.

God's concern for us is another foundational truth behind the altar ministry. God's invitation is all-inclusive. Anxieties negatively affect our lives, our health, our finances, our children, our community, our church and everything else that involves us. If God did not care for our welfare, prayer would be a waste of time.

Why is it necessary to tell God about our cares? Doesn't He already know all about our sorrows? Doesn't God love us? Isn't Jesus interceding on our behalf? Yes, that is all true. A logical question then arises—if God cares so much about us and knows all our troubles, why do we have to tell Him what He already knows? The answer isn't complicated. God respects our right to work out our own problems privately, if that is what we want to do. God is not officious; He doesn't impose Himself unless invited. He only helps those who ask for His assistance. God knows that people resent uninvited intrusions into their business. A wise father doesn't impose his help on his children unless it is wanted. Keeping our anxieties to ourselves sends a clear message to God: "Stay out of it. Don't interfere. I will handle it myself."

While some critics were complaining about the changes that I was making, others pointed to the full altars at every service and said, "Look at what God is doing in our church." Every two weeks we had to replace boxes of tissues in order to wipe away the tears of repentance, sorrow and joy. Others became impatient with altar calls at the end of every service. I replied, "As long as people keep coming to the altar and finding answers to their prayers, I will continue giving the invitation."

Just before leaving the church to become a minister-at-large, I asked the Sevenoaks congregation, "How many of you came to the altar with a specific need, seeking for divine help, and found it?" An usher estimated that about 700 hands were raised to testify of answered prayer. God granted many prayer requests. Some prayed for salvation, while others for sanctification, healing, employment, divine guidance, domestic tranquility and a multitude of other requests.

Another Bend in the Road

I knew from the beginning that my ministry would be short at Sevenoaks. This is typical for a pastor who succeeds a long-term, beloved pastor. Some told me, "If only you were more like our former pastor, we would get along much better." But God never asked me to be like someone else. In eternity, He will not ask me, "Why weren't you like Billy Graham or some other successful minister?" If I try to be someone else, the Lord will ask me, "Why weren't you the Al Runge I called and prepared for a unique ministry?" Long ago I made peace with God and myself.

I can say this to the credit of the elders: at the conclusion of my ministry, they had kept their promise to support my leadership, with very few exceptions.

One of my fears of growing old was that I would become useless and irrelevant. Only an exceptional church would call a senior citizen to be their pastor. I thought that the opportunities to minister would diminish with age. A district superintendent of my denomination confided in me while at lunch, "I would never recommend a pastor who is over fifty-five years of age for a church." It suddenly dawned on him that I was over fifty-five years of age at the time. With some embarrassment, he quickly backtracked by saying, "Of course, I would make an exception for you." Somehow I didn't quite believe him.

Fortunately not all district superintendents feel that way about older pastors. When I turned sixty-five, Harold Mangham, a district superintendent, asked me to consider becoming the interim pastor of an Alliance church in Washington state.

After six months of serving the church, an elder spoke critically of me in the board meeting. "Pastor, what are you doing for the large salary we are paying you?" It has always irritated me that some people undervalue the ministry of their pastor. I was getting a lower salary than at my last ministry and working harder. I explained that in addition to preaching three times every Sunday morning, supervising their staff and meeting with the church board every week, I was getting them ready for a permanent pastor. I was also trying to help them develop their future strategic plan. Lee and I had personally counseled over 350 key members in small groups. We were helping them to work through their grief and anger over their former pastor's leaving. I pointed out that only two families had left the church because they disagreed with the denomination's policy of disciplining pastors. It was not an easy job.

At the very next communion service, God gently whispered within my heart, "This is the last communion that you will serve as a full-time pastor of a church." Along with that insight, I felt the Lord's sympathetic understanding of how much the pastoral ministry meant to me. I knew He wasn't displeased with me, nor was He punishing me. It was just time to start a new chapter in my life.

Over the years, I have noticed many aging pastors who didn't seem to know when it was time to step aside. Trying to hold on to a church too long can be detrimental to a congregation. Years ago, I told my wife, who has a gift of spiritual wisdom, "Honey, let me know when it's time to step aside." The day came when Lee looked at me with that special knowing and loving look and said, "Honey, it's time for us to give up the full-time pastorate." She confirmed what the Lord had said to me.

Leaving the pastorate was as difficult for Lee as it was for me. Lee was a wonderful pastor's wife. We always did our best to put the glory of God and the welfare of His people first.

After fifty-one years of walking with Jesus, I retired from the pastorate. I then realized that my life would never be the same. Just after I became a Christian at fourteen years of age, I dreamt about becoming a pastor. I spent years of hard work and sacrifice to prepare myself for the ministry. I loved being the pastor of a congregation. Watching God working in lives was an exciting joy, but the day came when I had to face retirement.

CHAPTER THIRTEEN

Reassignment

For God's gifts and his call are irrevocable.
(Romans 11:29)

At first I was planning to entitle this chapter, "Entering My Sunset Years" because growing old meant a conclusion of meaningful living. Subconsciously, I was being influenced by the pessimistic worldview of growing old.

When I arrived in British Columbia, I suspected that because of my age, Sevenoaks would be my last ministry. As I was approaching my sixty-fifth birthday, I had a dream that was more like a nightmare. In my dream, I was skipping from place to place from east to west until I came to the Pacific Ocean. I was afraid to take another step because I might fall into the ocean and drown. I looked out over the ocean as the sun went down, leaving only a bright red streak across the horizon. The blackness of the night was setting in. Remembering that I had poor night vision, I sat down on the beach, hoping someone would come along and help guide me to safety. I cried out, "Is anyone there? Can anyone help me?" No one replied. I felt alone in the vastness of the cosmos. I woke up in a sweat. I realized that I was coming to the end of my life's journey. I was experiencing the natural fear of the unknown.

After I resigned from the Sevenoaks Alliance Church, Art Sauder, the church administrator, invited Lee and me to visit him at his home in White Rock by the Pacific Ocean.

After dinner, his wife, Maryann, suggested that we all take a walk on the beach. It was a beautiful evening. As we walked, I looked west over the ocean and watched the sunset. I got excited because the horizon looked exactly like it did in my dream, only I was not alone—my wife and friends were walking with me. The greatest joy of that moment was the sense of the presence of Jesus. In reality, I am not alone as I approach the sunset of my earthly journey.

My Identity Crisis

Retiring from the pastorate threw me into a personal identity crisis. I had spent nine years of plodding through schools to prepare myself to become a pastor. I diligently worked to restore, relocate and rebuild declining churches. Because the hand of the Lord was working with me, I experienced a good deal of success. I delighted in being called "pastor." The pastorate had become my life and identity. When people asked me, "What do you do for a living?" I gladly told them and delighted to add the size of my large congregation. The measure of my self-worth came from my vocation.

As a pastor, I focused all my energies on the daily demands of my duties. I kept some balance in my life by calculated neglect, putting aside everything except the most pressing issues. Rarely was I absent from my pulpit and my office. Day and night, I thought mostly about the challenges of my own ministry. My children joke about a distinctive family characteristic that sometimes drives our spouses to distraction. We call it "The Runge Focus." Once we get our minds on a project, everything else fades from view. All that we can think about and talk about is our project until it is completed. This is good and bad—good in that we get things accomplished, but bad because we can overlook other important concerns.

Once I was no longer a pastor of a church, I wondered, *Who am I, anyway? What can I do with all my free time?* No more secretaries to plan my schedules, no office to go to, no board meetings to chair, no counseling appointments, no deadlines for sermons. My first reaction was to waste time with trivial pursuits. I became a world-class couch potato, munching on snacks and watching television for hours. My wife kept trying to get me on the scales. Insisting I was fine, I argued, "Honey, I am at my top weight. I can't get any heavier. After all, I was born with just so many fat cells, and my body can't produce any new ones. They are all filled up to their limit. I am at a safe weight." I truly believed my theory until my doctor took my blood pressure and forced me on the scales. To my shock and chagrin, I had gained thirty-five pounds of unwanted, ugly fat, and my blood pressure was getting dangerously high. My hypothesis fell apart, compelling me to exercise and diet just in time to avoid a physical disaster.

I foolishly thought that my earthly life would soon come to a close. I had completed my church assignments well. All my children had left home and were married with children of their own. I wondered why was I still hanging around on earth. I wanted to be called to heaven, but the Lord Jesus spoke to me and said, "You have a number of years left to live. Once you get through them and look back, they will seem but a short time. Then will I come for you." I was happy to hear that from my Lord. I am looking forward to that day when He will come for me. I don't have to find heaven on my own.

It became obvious to me that the Lord had more for me to accomplish before I saw Him. Friends tell me that I am now living on borrowed time. The fact is that I am living on gifted time. Each day when I wake up still in this world, I recognize it is a gift from God. It brings new opportunities to serve Him.

God's Unchanging Plan

I got into reasonable shape; my health was good, my energy level high, and I longed to serve Jesus. I thought, *Why stay inactive when there is so much that needs to be done for the kingdom of God?* I adopted and echoed the prayer of A.W. Tozer, "Lord Jesus, save me from belonging to things, and puttering around the house wasting time."

I began searching for God's new purpose for my life. Some of my friends suggested that I find a hobby to occupy my free time. "Take up fishing and camping. Enjoy yourself. You have earned your retirement." But for me there was no greater joy to be found than serving Jesus. Nothing fulfills me as much as preaching the good news of Jesus. Why should I quit the ministry when I am still healthy, with the fire of God's Spirit burning in my heart to proclaim God's Word? God's call on my life did not end when I retired from the pastorate. I simply changed careers. I became a traveling minister-at-large. My senior years are overflowing with new and wonderful opportunities to serve the Lord.

God was not retiring me; He was just giving me a new assignment. At each juncture of my life's journey, God has had someone there to direct me. I did not have to look far for the answer. Lee developed a seminar called "Focusing Your Life." She encourages people to discover and write down their life-purpose statement. She put pressure on me to do mine. In her sweet and unassuming way, she got me going. Lee suggested that the first step to formulate my life purpose statement was to write out my epitaph. "How would you like to be remembered?" she asked me.

After giving it a great deal of thought, my mind went to one of the most astonishing verses in the Bible—Genesis 5:24:

"And Enoch walked with God: and he was not; for God took him" (KJV). If the Lord tarries, I want it to be said of me. "And Al Runge walked with God and he was not, for the Lord took him."

From that beginning, I began the arduous task of writing and rewriting my life-purpose statement until I came to the final product: "My life purpose is to testify of the faithfulness of Jesus Christ in my life in order to persuade others to trust Him with their lives."

Interestingly, God's purpose for me is in total agreement with my deepest longings. Once my purpose was clear, I began establishing priorities.

While a senior pastor, I had noticed some guest speakers who had a profoundly positive effect on my congregation. I remember one evangelist who insisted on singing solos off-key, performing silly magic tricks that didn't always work out and preaching long, mediocre messages. Yet when he gave the altar call, people rushed to the altar. One hundred twenty-five people came into the kingdom of God during his evangelistic crusade. God gave him a very special gift of evangelism.

Reminiscing on the effective gifts of so many guest speakers, I prayed, "Lord, if You want me to continue preaching and teaching, grant me the gifts necessary to be a blessing to a church in a short amount of time."

God then gave me two promises from His Word: "They will still bear fruit in old age, they will stay fresh and green, proclaiming, 'The LORD is upright; he is my Rock, and there is no wickedness in him' " (Psalm 92:15). And "You did not choose me, but I chose you and appointed you to go and bear fruit—fruit that will last" (John 15:16).

Without the financial and professional support of a church, I decided to be proactive. My first priority was to develop new skills. A church no longer provided a secretary for me, and since I lacked the money to hire one, I decided to do the job myself. I wanted to get the word out that I was available for ministry. I purchased a computer, a laser printer and software that taught me typing. Through trial and error, and with the help of my knowledgeable friend, David Philips, who had once worked on my pastoral staff, I was soon able to accomplish some simple tasks. Within a few months, I was typing at the rate of twenty-five to thirty words a minute. The sense of achievement encouraged me to go on. In a short time, I was producing letterheads and brochures on my own. I had found a useful hobby after all! I got on the Internet and I started sending out e-mail, notifying district superintendents and missionaries of my availability for ministry. In response to my letters, a number of invitations began trickling in. A whole new era opened up for me.

My next step was assessing my talents and abilities for their benefit to the kingdom of God. I recognized the gifts that God had already given me to bring healing to broken churches. At the time I wasn't sure if my abilities were usable in a worldwide context.

Lee said to me, "When you retire, I don't want to be taking you to the airport and being left behind." I promised her that I would take her with me wherever I went. God has used her to bring a blessing of purposefulness to many lives.

A New Beginning

Soon after I resigned from the pastorate, a group of Israeli and Palestinian missionaries invited me to minister to them at their annual retreat. In addition, I was given the opportunity to preach at Hebrew Messianic Assemblies and a Palestinian church in the old city of Jerusalem.

My wife and I accepted the invitation, knowing that we would have to raise the money for the trip since we were not financially able to pay for it by ourselves. We needed the money by a certain day or we would be forced to cancel. On the very last day of our deadline, Peter Hildebrandt asked me out for coffee at McDonald's. Over a 27-cent senior cup of coffee, he explained the purpose of his invitation, "Last night my wife Mary and I were in bed reading the newspaper. We saw an ad for a round trip to Israel on Air Canada for $1,500. 'I've got an idea,' I said to Mary. 'We will never go to Israel, but let's send Al and Lee.' " He then handed me a check for $3,200. I have come to understand that if God wants us to do a job for His kingdom, He will provide the necessary resources.

Spending time in the land of my ancestors was an emotional experience. We felt completely at home. Lee and I loved to go to Yehudah Street and sit for hours at an outdoor café. Once we got a table, it belonged to us for the rest of the evening. Those cafés were the center of the social life of the people. Once people discovered we were Jewish, they tried to talk us into immigrating to Israel along with our children and grandchildren.

We also shared in the sorrows of Israel. On one occasion, we were waiting at a table to order our meal when a police car, siren wailing, drove up onto the sidewalk. I couldn't make out what the policeman was shouting over his speaker, but I watched everyone get up and quickly walk away. Finally I made out one word, "Bomb, bomb, bomb." We also left in haste.

Someone had forgotten his briefcase and left it under a table. The police, not wanting to take any chances, blew it up. When we found out that it was a false alarm we came back with everyone else to finish our meal. I was impressed that no one panicked.

I ministered to both Israeli and Palestinian missionaries. I had the opportunity to preach at a number of Messianic Assemblies where Christ is preached in the Hebrew. Multitudes of Jews from former communist countries are placing their faith in Jesus and at the same time retaining their Jewish identity. Lee and I had the pleasure of sharing the Sabbath meal at a Messianic kibbutz. All over the world there are assemblies of Jews springing up to worship Jesus, the Jewish Messiah and the Savior of the world. I also spoke in a Palestinian church in the old city of Jerusalem. Thirteen Arabic young people committed their lives to the Lord Jesus.

The time we spent in Israel opened our eyes to the troubles of the Israelis. Two days before we were to leave Israel, we were planning to take a bus to see the Hebrew University. At the last minute a Jordanian missionary persuaded us to go with him instead to an Arabic restaurant on the Mount of Olives overlooking the city of Jerusalem. Later we heard that the very bus we might have taken was blown up by a suicidal terrorist. A collective grief, sadness and despair filled the nation. Everyone spoke of a desire for peace.

The day after the bombing, we listened to the sorrow of our waitress, who had just been released from her tour of duty in the Israeli army. She talked of her desire for peace as tears filled her eyes. I said, "One day the *Ha Sar Shalom* [the Prince of Peace] will return to bring lasting peace to Israel."

"May He come soon," she said.

To that sentiment, we all said, "Amen!"

On September 13, 1993, after signing the Israeli–Palestinian peace agreement, Yitzhak Rabin, the Israeli prime minister, gave a speech at the White House. He expressed the view of the majority of Israelis, who desire peace:

> We the soldiers who have returned from battles stained with blood; we who have seen our relatives and friends killed before our eyes; we who have attended their funerals and cannot look in the eyes of their parents; we who have come from a land where parents bury their children; we who have fought against you, the Palestinians—we say to you today, in a loud and a clear voice: enough of blood and tears. Enough.[1]

The Jewish prophets predicted that only the Messiah will bring in everlasting peace. The day will come when Israel and the world will experience real peace.

> For to us a child is born,
> to us a son is given,
> and the government will be on his shoulders.
> And he will be called
> Wonderful Counselor, Mighty God,
> Everlasting Father, Prince of Peace.
> Of the increase of his government and peace
> there will be no end.
> He will reign on David's throne
> and over his kingdom,
> establishing and upholding it
> with justice and righteousness
> from that time on and forever.
> The zeal of the LORD Almighty
> will accomplish this. (Isaiah 9:6-7)

We stayed in Jerusalem at a missionary guest house. On July 30, 1995, Lee and I went to the Western Wall, once called the Wailing Wall. In my diary, I recorded the prayer I prayed for Israel at the wall:

> O Heavenly Father,
> I come to you in the name of Your Son, Jesus.
> Now I understand why He wept over Jerusalem when He said,
>
> > "O Jerusalem, Jerusalem, you who kill the prophets and stone those sent to you, how often I have longed to gather your children together, as a hen gathers her chicks under her wings, but you were not willing. Look, your house is left to you desolate. For I tell you, you will not see me again until you say, 'Blessed is he who comes in the name of the Lord.' " (Matthew 23:37-39)
>
> Lord, You are merciful. Remember Your covenant with Abraham, Isaac and Jacob and Your promise of a new covenant with the house of Judah and with the house of Israel. You promised to give them a new heart and write Your laws on their hearts. Oh Lord Jesus, please call to Your Spirit, the Breath of Life, that He may breathe upon these slain, that they may live.

I closed my prayer in the Hebrew name of Jesus, Yeshua. I felt a release in my spirit, because I sensed God heard me. I believe that I had prayed according to the will of God even as multitudes of others have done. The day will come when all Israel shall be saved.

A Confirmation of My Ministry

I wanted to be His faithful servant, but I had a concern about my value to the kingdom of God. I wondered if God would still use me. My fears were soon relieved. After returning from Israel, we received a letter of commendation from David Lauffer, the field chairman of Israel.

> Al exercises an unusually anointed preaching gift. The response to the messages he delivered in various Israeli contexts (both Jewish and Arab) was extraordinary in terms of personal decisions for Christ and for total commitment to His will. Our Israeli field appreciated his perceptive insights in strategic planning.

We were then invited to Ecuador to minister to the missionaries at their yearly retreat. While there, I was asked to speak at a church in Quito that was going through a very difficult time that had led to a serious division within the congregation.

Everyone was hurting. I felt the atmosphere of depression in the air. In my message I related my experience at Omaha, where I led a broken and divided church into becoming a vital and growing church located on twenty-six acres of land. Not only was that church blessed with significant growth, but also those who left with the former pastor to start another church in the community. Christ now has two large churches, instead of just one, that minister to 6,000 people each week.

I warned the congregation against grieving the Holy Spirit by bitterness and speaking evil against those who left. I encouraged them to forgive those who had hurt them and remain positive in their ministry. Since I had to speak through an interpreter, I wasn't sure if my ministry was helpful. My doubts evaporated when I asked the congregation to indicate their commitment to forgive, to forget the past hurts and to stick with their church. Just about everyone raised his hand in agreement.

After my message I gave an invitation for salvation. The icing on the cake was seeing those who came forward to receive Christ as their Savior, especially as this was not an evangelistic message. God sealed the truth with His blessing. Later I was told that this was the first time in many months that anyone had come forward to receive Christ.

In the afternoon, I met with the members of the new board and encouraged them to keep on loving those who had left, to speak well of them and to keep the channels of communication open with them. I admonished them to consider the new congregation not as a rival but as a sister church in Christ. Since that time, I have heard of the increase of growth and blessing on that church. Three years later, the two congregations met at a service of reconciliation. Their theme was "two congregations—one church." My experience in Ecuador confirmed that I still have a meaningful ministry.

Lee and I have the opportunity to visit and minister to many of the mission fields of the world. What we are discovering overseas thrills our hearts, but at the same time it bothers me that I was so shortsighted in the past. I should have had a broader vision of God's kingdom. Occasionally I preached on missions, but I could have done far more. I pushed for missionary support and raised a lot of money, but not nearly enough. I have come to appreciate the dedication and sacrificial work of our missionaries.

With all my training and experience in evangelism, church growth and strategic planning, I realized I still had something of value to offer. In addition to the gift of bringing health to broken churches, the Lord has given me the gift of evangelism. Everywhere I speak and give an invitation for salvation and for the Spirit-filled life, people respond positively.

I was invited by Campus Crusade in Poland to come and speak at their university winter retreat. Students came from all over Poland, the Ukraine, Russia, the city of Minsk in Belarus and Lithuania. They had all grown up under atheistic communism. From the time they entered elementary school they were taught all the logical arguments against the existence of God. From the beginning I decided not to approach them from an apologetic viewpoint. Rather, I felt led to share my personal experience of walking with Jesus for fifty-six years.

The results were more than gratifying. At the end of the conference, I asked the students, "How many of you have made a definite commitment to receive Jesus either as Savior or the Lord of your life for the first time this week?" Many hands were raised. These students are the elite of their countries, studying international banking, business, law, political science and medicine. They will permeate their societies with a Christian witness.

We spent eight days with the students. Lee and I loved to be the recipients of the genuine affection of those precious students. They told us, "We have never before met a mature Christian like you." "We wish we had grandparents like you who would have taught us the ways of God." "We never thought of listening to the voice of God before you spoke."

One of the Polish students asked me to pray for him because all his life he was taught to hate the Jews. I was the first Jew that he ever met. God released him from his attitude and we hugged each other as brothers.

Later I received an e-mail from a Campus Crusade worker in Poland. He informed me that one of the young ladies who received Jesus as her Savior had led three of her university friends to Christ.

God is still using us everywhere we go to speak about our Lord. Whether I am a pastor or not, my life purpose can still be fulfilled in other ways. I can share many valuable experiences of the faithfulness of Jesus in my life. We have traveled to Israel, the West Bank, Ecuador, Italy, Thailand, Hong Kong, Poland and Indonesia, sharing testimony of His grace. I have spoken at colleges, seminaries, banquets and churches. Nothing thrills me as much as watching people come forward to the prayer altar to commit their lives to Christ in response to my story.

The best compliment ever paid me was at a course in strategic planning at Fuller Seminary. At the end of our course students expressed what they admired in each of their fellow students. One young man said about me, "Al Runge is the youngest person in our class." I was at least thirty years older in age than the oldest student there! To do our best for our Lord, we must never stop learning.

Note

1. Taken from a speech given by Yitzhak Rabin at the White House.

CHAPTER FOURTEEN

Counting My Blessings

The LORD your God has blessed you in all the work of your hands. He has watched over your journey through this vast desert. These forty years the LORD your God has been with you, and you have not lacked anything. (Deuteronomy 2:7)

What I did not know at the time that I came to Christ was that there were many earthly blessings waiting for me. In Mark 10:29-30, Jesus told Peter,

> Assuredly, I say to you, there is no one who has left house or brothers or sisters or father or mother or wife or children or lands, for My sake and the gospel's, who shall not receive a hundredfold now in this time—houses and brothers and sisters and mothers and children and lands, with persecutions—and in the age to come, eternal life. (NKJV)

The only thing I knew for sure was that Jesus had taken me by the hand and was leading me into an unknown future.

The Blessing of Godly Children

> "I will pour out my Spirit on your offspring,
> and my blessing on your descendants."
>
> (Isaiah 44:3)

"The children of your servants will live
in your presence;
their descendants will be established before you."

(Psalm 102:28)

The question was asked by the ancient rabbis, "Why did God speak of Himself as the God of Abraham, the God of Isaac and the God of Jacob? Why did He not speak collectively of all of them and say, 'I am the God of Abraham, Isaac and Jacob?' "

An ancient rabbi answered this question well: "Each and every person must know God for Himself." A child cannot live by the faith and experience of his parents. True faith is a very personal matter. Yet the father is responsible to pass on his spiritual heritage to his children and thereby bring down divine blessing upon his future generations.

Moses commanded the parents of Israel, "Only be careful, and watch yourselves closely so that you do not forget the things your eyes have seen or let them slip from your heart as long as you live. Teach them to your children and to their children after them" (Deuteronomy 4:9).

Many times over the years I shared my testimony with my children. I told them how I marvel at God's faithfulness and love not only for me, but also for them. I did my best to teach them to trust God for their futures.

My life story would not be complete if I did not share the blessings that He has bestowed on my children. He has blessed all my children with intelligence and significant abilities. Robin, my older daughter, achieved a Master's degree in counseling. My son David has a bachelor's degree in atmospheric sciences and a Master's degree in environmental engineering and worked himself up from an enlisted serviceman to a captain in the United States Air Force. My son Peter has a Master of Divinity degree and is working on his doctorate in leadership development. My youngest daughter, Sharon, has a Bachelor's degree in biblical studies. They all love the Lord and are now active in the church along with their families.

I want to share something special from the lives of my four children. I will start with my firstborn, Robin.

A Daughter's Tribute

"Honor your father and your mother." (Exodus 20:12)

All through my ministry, I have had my critics. Thank God that they were very few in contrast with the multitudes of my supporters. More important than what people thought of me is what my children think of me now. Robin went through a period of rebellion, and for a time I thought I had lost her, but God restored her.

For one Father's Day greeting, Robin wrote me a letter that I will always cherish.

> Dear Dad,
>
> I am sitting in a seminar called "Creativity in Ministry" by Howard Hendricks. He reminds me of you in some ways.
>
> I want to tell you how much I admire you for your dedication to God and your creativity in ministry.
>
> There are many other qualities in your life I am trying to emulate in mine. I admire your strong faith in God, your intelligence and your determination. It is great to see the way you tackle big

problems and solve them and the way you enjoy your life and work. I used to think I was mostly like Mom, but the older I get the more I see how much I am like you. I think the way you do in many ways. Some of my life goals are similar to yours—serving God and working with people. Sometimes I wish I could make more money, but I think the most important thing is that my work is pleasing with God. I know that you feel the same way, since there were times you turned away from making more money in order to do what God wanted you to do. I am proud to have a father like you. Have a wonderful Father's Day.
Love, Robin

A Son's Inquiry

"Listen to your father, who gave you life."

(Proverbs 23:22)

We can always depend on God to give us direction for our children when they ask us for it. Some years ago, my son David was in the Navy. He served on the *Eisenhower* aircraft carrier for four years. During the Iranian hostage crisis, his ship was stationed battle-ready for nine months in the Indian Ocean. On the way back to the States, his ship stopped to visit Israel. In the middle of the night, my phone rang, waking me up from a sound sleep at about 2 o'clock in the morning.

David was calling me collect from Israel to ask for my advice. He informed me that his captain had called him to his cabin that afternoon and offered him a $10,000 bonus to reenlist for four more years, promising my son shore duty in the state of Maine for his next tour of duty. Anticipating David would accept his generous offer, the captain had booked him on a mail plane flying back to the States the following day.

David said, "Dad, I am sick of the living on a ship. I don't know if I should reenlist or not. I will do whatever you tell me."

I asked for a moment to wake up and ask the Lord for wisdom. I was tempted to give him some contemporary wisdom, "David, you are an adult. I trust you to do whatever is best for you," but I knew David wanted more than common sense—he wanted to know God's will. So I prayed, "Lord, You know the future and what is best for David. How should I deal with his question?"

Within seconds God gave me the wisdom to answer him. "David," I asked, "when is your enlistment up?"

He replied, "In about three months."

"This is the counsel that I believe God has given me for you. It is unwise to do anything while under pressure, even for $10,000. Serve your time out, get your honorable discharge and come home to think about your future."

"OK, Dad, I will do what you say," he assured me.

Four weeks later, I received a letter from my son. "Dear Dad, thank you for your advice. It was truly from God. The mail plane I was assigned to fly on to Maine was lost at sea, and there were no survivors." If David had reenlisted, he would have died at sea, and three of our precious granddaughters would not have been born. What if I hadn't sought for guidance from God? My grief and guilt would have been unbearable. I am very glad that David has such high regard for me.

A Son's Discovery

"I have heard of You by the hearing of the ear,
but now my eye sees You." (Job 42:5, NKJV)

It is important for our children to come to know God for themselves. Peter insisted on enrolling in an expensive Christian liberal arts college even though I told him that I could not afford to help him. He ended my arguments by telling me that the Lord was leading him to go there. He said, "You always said that if we do God's will, He will provide the money needed." He then quoted Philippians 4:19, "And my God will meet all your needs according to his glorious riches in Christ Jesus." I gave in and wished him the best.

Peter graduated with a very large school debt. My Canadian church board hired him to assist the youth pastor, which enabled him to come to Canada. He wasn't being paid enough money to pay off his debt and go on to seminary. We estimated it would take him many years to afford to go on with his ministerial education.

A wealthy lady in our church took special notice of Peter's spiritual giftedness and dedication to ministry. One day she took him aside and asked him, "Peter, do you have any college debts?"

"Yes!"

"How much do you owe?"

"About $13,000."

She asked him if that was in U.S. currency or Canadian. Peter informed her it was all in U.S. funds. She took out her calculator, figured out the exchange rate and without blinking an eye wrote out a check to cover it all. He was able to go on to seminary.

Later Peter said with a knowing smile, "Dad, I have always admired how God provided for you. Now I know for myself that He is also my provider."

A Daughter's Miracle

> "He settles the barren woman in her home
> as a happy mother of children.
> Praise the LORD." (Psalm 113:9)

My daughter Sharon and her husband wanted a child to love. They had unsuccessfully tried to have children for five years. After an exploratory operation, the surgeon informed them that Sharon had less than a ten percent chance of having a baby in the first year after the operation, and less than a one percent chance in the second year. Her physician father-in-law told me that in his professional opinion there wasn't any possibility for her to conceive. Months were slipping by without any indication of a pregnancy.

They were preparing to adopt a child when I suggested they come to the prayer altar after a service. With tears and hearts thankful to God for His love, they made their request known to Him. Ten months later Sharon gave birth to Rebecca, a beautiful baby girl.

A few months later, Sharon called my wife. "Mom, keep this secret for a while, but I am pregnant again!" Luke and Sharon decided that since they had had to wait nearly six years for their first child, they should get started right away for a second one. God granted them a second blessing, their daughter Marie. Two years later Sharon gave birth to her third child, Ruth. God delights in answering the prayers of His children. God has not only blessed me with four godly children, but also with eleven wonderful grandchildren.

There is no greater joy for me than to realize that all my children and their spouses love Jesus. All my grandchildren are growing up in good churches where they are being nurtured in the Lord. If I had only succeeded in building large churches for the kingdom of God and yet lost my own children to a secular, immoral life, all my achievements would be of little value in my old age.

The Blessing of a Godly Wife

I would not have godly children if it weren't for my godly wife, their godly mother. Robin, the songwriter and poet of the family, wrote a poem in honor of her mother. She called it "Mom."

Soft wind that blows the sails
The calm that heals the storm
The sunrise without fail
The soul with love and warmth

A peace that comes from knowing
That God is always there
A simple faith in Jesus
Gives wings to all her prayers

You never asked for glory
You never cared for fame
You gave yourself to others
You loved us all the same

I thank God for you, Mom
I've always known you cared

You have stood behind us all
Like an angel unaware

There is no greater love than this
That we would live for others
There is no greater blessing than
A kind and godly mother

Robin very precisely described her mother. Lee is a totally unselfish woman, completely committed to God, His people, our children and me. Lee freely admits that she isn't perfect, but in our eyes she comes as close as possible for a human being saved by grace.

Our Family's Vision

"But as for me and my household, we will serve the LORD." (Joshua 24:15)

In August of 1998, our entire family met together. All twenty-one of us enjoyed each other's company, and our eleven grandchildren got to know each other. The main purpose of the gathering was to write out a family purpose statement. We sang praises to our Lord, prayed for wisdom and sought the mind of God. When we got done we all agreed on this statement: "To glorify God by enlarging His kingdom in the world, beginning with our own family, and then by compassionate reaching out to the world as anointed and significant leaders."

We then sealed our vision statement by presenting our vision to the Lord for His blessing. On my mother's side there had been rabbis for many past generations. It is our desire that if He tarries there will be many men and women of God from our line who will faithfully proclaim Jesus, the true Messiah of Israel and the Savior of the world.

The Blessing of God's Generosity

As I was growing older, I began worrying about financial security. God gave me a promise from Isaiah 46:4: "Even to your old age and gray hairs I am he, I am he who will sustain you. I have made you and I will carry you; I will sustain you and I will rescue you."

On December 26, 1983, I had just turned fifty-five years of age. All kinds of strange sensations and insights were hitting me hard, such as the realization that my lifetime was running out. I recorded this prayer in my journal:

> Dear Lord Jesus,
> I read the obituaries every now and then and notice that many younger people than I am are dying; it makes me realize my own mortality. I am not questioning my eternal life or the heaven You have promised me. My heart is settled on those issues. My fear is being considered too old for opportunities to serve You. Although I am still healthy, each day I expect to feel some of the pains of growing old. Gloomy questions sometimes trouble me. What if I have a heart attack or a stroke? What if I die and leave my wife alone in Canada with no pension or money to survive? In my present financial state, I am not in any condition to get sick or die. Help us, oh Lord. Amen.

I was trying not to complain. I believed God would somehow and some way take care of me, because He is faithful, but in 1983 my shaky faith was being tested. My best reward from ministry was not monetary. My satisfaction came from seeing the churches under my leadership prosper. But unfortunately, I had no financial resources for our future security.

The promise of Hebrews 13:5-6 comforted me with the assurance of the Lord's presence. "Keep your lives free from the love of money and be content with what you have, because God has said, 'Never will I leave you; never will I forsake you.' So we say with confidence, 'The Lord is my helper; I will not be afraid. What can man do to me?' "

I can honestly say that while I did not love money, I understood that without it, life would be difficult for Lee and me, especially in our old age. I also recognized that in order to be free to serve the Lord in my old age, I would need sufficient financial resources.

One sunny afternoon I took a walk along Jasper Avenue, deeply troubled over my financial condition. I literally felt physical pain from my stress and fear for the future. From the corner of my eye, I glanced at an elderly man approaching me. He said, "God will take care of you in your old age." He then walked away. I had never seen him before that encounter, and I never saw him after. No human being could possibly know my inner despair of growing old or dying in poverty. He was a messenger from God. Whether he was an angel from heaven or a Christian obeying the leading of the Lord, I can't say. Either way, he encouraged me exceedingly. I prefer to think he was an angel from God. I wish I had had the presence of mind to invite him out for a cup of coffee and a chat. There are a lot of questions I would like to ask an angel!

I began considering what God did financially for ancient Job after his trials were over. Job's friends and relatives came to him and each one gave him a piece of gold and of silver. I said off the cuff, "Lord, I know You can influence people to do that for me as well." I soon forgot my remarks to the Lord.

About a month later, I was invited to speak at Southview Alliance Church in Calgary. One of their members phoned me, inviting my wife and me to stay overnight with them while we were in Calgary. We accepted his gracious invitation.

Before bedtime, my host asked me, "Do you have any gold?"

"No," I replied.

He went into another room and soon came back with a shoe box full of gold coins and ounce-size gold bars. "Which do you like better?" he asked.

"The gold coins," I responded.

"Take one," he said, thrusting the box toward me.

I was caught by surprise and didn't know what to say. I blurted out, "Why are you giving me gold? I'm not Billy Graham!" I thought, *Who ever gives gold to pastors?*

He said, "Take *two* gold coins." (I guess it was a good line.) Then he asked me if I had any silver. Again I replied negatively. He then gave me six ounces of silver. He said, "You can no longer say, 'Silver and gold have I none.' "

"Why are you giving me the silver and gold?" I asked.

He replied, "Because God told me to give them to you."

Then I remembered my off-the-cuff prayer concerning a gift of gold and silver. Those gold coins and six-ounce bars of silver became symbols of God's faithfulness to me in the years ahead.

There are a number of hindrances to prayer. My biggest obstacle is false assumptions. Sometimes I presume to know the mind of God even before I pray. From time to time I am so convinced that God is going to turn down my request that I foolishly don't even ask for it.

I told my wife I was considering asking God for a specific amount of assets by the time we retired. She laughed at my *chutzpah* (nerve) and said, "There is no way that will ever happen!" I asked God for it anyway but then felt greedy. So I apologized and took back my request. I did this three times. Finally I said, "Lord, I don't know if I am being too materialistic or if this request offends You, so I will let You decide. You know my heart better than I do, so I will let my request stand."

Through experience I have come to understand that our heavenly Father will not give us anything that will hurt us. Since I can't read God's mind, I will not hesitate to present all of my requests to Him. The Bible invites us to do just that, in Philippians 4:6-7, "Do not be anxious about anything, but in everything, by prayer and petition, with thanksgiving, present your requests to God. And the peace of God, which transcends all understanding, will guard your hearts and your minds in Christ Jesus."

We honor God by asking Him for the impossible. There is a story about Alexander the Great, who wanted to honor a faithful servant. The king told the servant to go to his treasurer and tell him what he wanted for a reward. Later, the treasurer came to Alexander complaining about the huge sum the servant requested. "This unreasonable reward is too much."

Alexander replied, "You don't understand; my servant has paid me a great compliment, for he acknowledges my greatness."

Ten years later when I left the pastorate, God had answered my prayer. He gave me the exact amount of assets that I had requested from Him. We own a home without a mortgage. We have no debts. We can afford to retire completely in our senior years, if we so desire. I should not have been surprised by God's generosity. I went through nine years of education by faith and finished without any debt. All my children graduated with university degrees; three of my four children have earned master's degrees without any school debts. Our family never went hungry or became homeless. I was never unemployed. Every church where I had candidated called me to be their pastor. Even when I was sixty-two years old, I received a call to pastor the largest Alliance church in Canada.

I am glad that the Lord is merciful and long suffering with me. God keeps His promises. "And my God will meet all your needs according to his glorious riches in Christ Jesus" (Philippians 4:19).

The Blessing of Communicating with God

I don't want you to get a wrong impression about my prayer life. I am not a mighty prayer warrior—far from it. I often busy myself with too many activities and neglect prayer. My wandering mind frequently distracts me during my prayer time and I can easily fall asleep on my knees.

Although God has answered many of my prayers over the years, I am still learning about the true meaning of prayer. I understood the significance of prayer for my life, but I did not know how important prayer is to God. I had a false presumption about prayer. I never analyzed it consciously, but I felt it to be true and operated my life by it. I presumed that prayer was solely meant for my benefit, to get me out of trouble, to provide material things for me and to give me successes in the ministry.

After leaving my church I threw a pity party for myself. I was reflecting back over all the real and imaginary mistakes I had ever made in life, being very hard on myself. Out of the blue, my heavenly Father interrupted my depressing, self-centered and condemning thoughts with a penetrating question, "Aren't you talking to Me anymore?"

Such an inquiry of love and the emotion I felt behind the words caught me completely by surprise. God's question penetrated like a laser beam burning its way through all my ego defense systems right into my heart. It was beyond my human comprehension that Almighty God simply wanted to dialogue with such an insignificant creature made of dust like me, but He does. The All-Sufficient One desires our fellowship.

In the past, I had feared that just talking to God would be dangerous. What if I said something foolish or selfish or contrary to God's perfect will? I did not want to offend a holy God with my unwise chatter. I thought that my prayers had to be formulated with good theological concepts and high-sounding words in order to acknowledge the dignity and majesty of God. I have come to realize that God is my Father and that Jesus is not only my Lord, but also my closest and dearest Friend. Certainly I must make every effort to speak respectfully to Him, but I now realize He sees my heart's intentions and motivations. He knows that I love Him and I know my place as His servant.

The Lord and I often chat together. My major discovery about prayer is that it is the channel for fellowship with God. The apostle John tells us in First John 1:3, "We proclaim to you what we have seen and heard, so that you also may have fellowship with us. And our fellowship is with the Father and with his Son, Jesus Christ."

Prayer is more than giving a personal shopping list to God; it is having fellowship with Him. Our Lord created us to dialogue with Him. Before Adam fell in sin, God walked and talked with Him in the cool of each day. He desires that we walk humbly with Him.

The Blessing of Genuine Friendships

Within Jewish culture, a true friend can be as close as a blood relative. The older I get, the more I realize how much I appreciate true friends, people who stand by me in every kind of situation. One of my fears of growing older was becoming isolated from the people I knew and loved. Some expect a retired pastor to leave his church, his friends and his home and move away to another town. No other profession places such an expectation on its members.

After we left Sevenoaks Alliance Church, we remained in Abbotsford, but out of respect for the rules of our denomination, we stayed away from the church to allow a new senior pastor time to establish his leadership with the congregation. We waited nearly two years for the church leadership to find my successor. Since no candidates were in sight, I suggested that the elders consider my former Omaha youth pastor, Richard Porter.

Rick had become my youth pastor right out of seminary over twenty years ago. His first two years in Omaha were difficult for him as he struggled to discover his gifted place in the ministry. One day he admitted to me that he wasn't cut out to be a youth pastor. With tearful eyes, he began questioning his very call to ministry.

I told him, "Rick, don't get discouraged. Let's find out what gifts God has given you." I gave him various opportunities. I asked him to preach at a Sunday evening service. I was astonished at his remarkable gift of preaching God's Word—he did it clearly and powerfully. Even as a novice, he had the gifts of preaching and leadership. I suggested he look for a position as a senior pastor. His parents, who were long-time members of the church, were not very pleased with me. They had hoped he and his wife and their grandchildren would stay in Omaha.

Over the years our respect for each other has grown. Under his leadership the church is growing again and he has won the respect and hearts of the people.

Pastor Rick and the elders unanimously invited us back into the active membership of the congregation. When the pastor publicly welcomed us, the congregation broke out in applause. Recently at lunch I said to him, "Rick, if I knew that one day you would become my pastor, I would have treated you much better." We both had a good laugh.

We are happy to have a church home in our senior years. Sevenoaks Alliance Church is a place where we feel respected and loved. So Lee and I now feel quite satisfied that we completed our assignment to bring beneficial change for the future good of the Sevenoaks Alliance Church.

The Blessing of Usefulness

There is no greater joy for me than to discover that I have been a blessing to others. Everywhere Lee and I travel, we meet people who tell us that we were a blessing to them. I believe the Lord planned those encouraging surprises for us. I was invited to speak to a thousand students at Nyack College three times a day for five days. Dr. Bill Saxby, the head of the psychology department at Nyack, introduced me to the faculty and students. He said, "I don't think Pastor Runge knows the blessing he has been to me and my wife, Pat. One Sunday she invited me to hear Pastor Runge. He spoke on faith and works. He made me so angry that all I said to Pat that evening was, 'Pass the ketchup.' Thinking my silence was anger toward her, Pat's eyes filled with tears.

"I took her home without saying a word. I was brought up in a church that taught that good works got us into heaven. That night I struggled until I discovered peace through the grace of God. So let me introduce my friend and spiritual mentor, Pastor Al Runge."

We hugged and the students cheered.

The Word of God speaks of the honor of a good name: "A good name is more desirable than great riches; to be esteemed is better than silver or gold" (Proverbs 22:1).

Each night the altar, the aisles and even the platform were filled with praying students. At the end of the week the college chaplain handed me a check and told me that the students gave me the largest love offering ever given to a special speaker in the long history of the college. The important accomplishment was not in the offering but in the hearts of the students who found Christ and those who discovered the secret of the Spirit-filled life. God is still encouraging Lee and me every step of our way.

The Blessing of Heaven

The Jewish prophet Isaiah wrote, "Your eyes will see the king in his beauty and view a land that stretches afar" (Isaiah 33:17). From the very first day that I received Jesus as my Savior, I anticipated the time I, along with God's people, shall see Him face-to-face and enjoy His fellowship forever. The atmosphere of heaven is one of perfect love, and I had a foretaste of that love when I became a Christian. I entered into the wonderful family of God's people. I will always remember Christians like Donald Ebner, Jr. He was just a few years older than I was and came from an entirely different background. He was born and raised in a wealthy Christian family; Donald lived the style of life that was beyond my wildest imagination.

At the end of World War II, he was honorably discharged from military service as a fighter pilot. I envied his refinement and polished personality, yet Donald was not a snob. Though I was younger and came from a poor Jewish family he befriended me.

Donald invited me to spend a day at his family's summer home on Rockaway Beach. It was a fun day for me. Everything was perfect—the cool ocean breeze, the saltwater, the sandy beach, the barbecue; it was the good life, the kind of life I could have gotten used to quite easily.

After a swim, Donald rushed into the house, followed by his beautiful fiancée. He opened the refrigerator door and took out an apple without asking for permission. Between bites, he asked his dad for the car keys and some money to take his girl out. Without a blink of an eye, his father took out his wallet, gave him a $20 bill and asked him if he needed more. I was lucky to get a quarter from my dad. His favorite lines were "Does money grows on trees?" and "What do you think, I am made of money?"

After sundown, I said good-bye to Donald and his family. I left the good life at the beach and took a bus and subway for a two-hour trip back to the sweltering inner city. The Ebners liked me but they were not my parents. I had no right to open up their refrigerator and help myself to a snack. I was only a one-time guest, not a son.

As I was returning to the city on the subway train, I held a pity party for myself until I sensed the presence of the Lord. He understood my situation. Jesus also experienced poverty while on earth. I realized that I wasn't returning to my true eternal home in heaven, but only to my temporary address with the bedbugs and cockroaches on Pulaski Street in Brooklyn.

I knew I had a heavenly Father and a Savior who were busy getting my real home ready for me. Jesus made a promise to His disciples in John 14:2-3: "In My Father's house are many dwelling places; if it were not so, I would have told you; for I go to prepare a place for you. And if I go and prepare a place for you, I will come again, and receive you to Myself; that where I am, there you may be also" (NASB).

Right there in the subway train on my way home to Brooklyn, I had a foretaste of heaven, my eternal home.

CHAPTER FIFTEEN

Concluding Reflections

You know with all your heart and soul that not one of all the good promises the LORD your God gave you has failed. Every promise has been fulfilled; not one has failed. But just as every good promise of the LORD your God has come true, so the LORD will bring on you all the evil he has threatened, until he has destroyed you from this good land he has given you. (Joshua 23:14-15)

The Afterglow Years

The word "afterglow" signifies to me achievement, satisfaction, fulfillment and all that goes with those pleasant attainments. The prophet Joel wrote that when the Holy Spirit would be poured out, "Your old men will dream dreams, your young men will see visions" (Joel 2:28). My take on that verse is that the old will look back over their lives with satisfaction by remembering God's blessings.

The greatest blessing that I have experienced has been the undying and faithful love of my Lord Jesus. As a teenage Christian, I expected to be perfect and fully knowledgeable about God and the Christian life by the age of thirty. When that did not happen I thought, *Maybe by the time I reach forty, I will truly know it all.* Now that I have passed threescore and ten years of age, I am still a learner. I am far from being a genius, but I have the Holy Spirit, who is a patient Teacher. From the time He first gave me insights to the gospel of Christ even to this day, He keeps on teaching me.

God's Endless Love

My journey through life with the Lord Jesus has covered almost seven decades. With the passing of each year, I continue to discover that there is always more to learn about God's love.

Recently I said to God, "Lord, You have been so good to me all through the years. What can I do to show You my gratitude?" I expected some enormous project would come to mind or a request for a special sacrificial offering. Instead He simply spoke to my heart with His familiar voice—"Just let Me love you!"

The greatest discovery of my life is that Jesus loves us fully and completely. God is just as interested in me now that I am a senior, nearing the end of my life, as when I started out as a young man with a whole life ahead of me. Jesus saves us not for how much He can get out of us, but how much He can benefit us.

The Bible explains, "We love him, because he first loved us" (1 John 4:19, KJV), and in Ephesians 3:17-19, the Bible tells us:

> So that Christ may dwell in your hearts through faith. And I pray that you, being rooted and established in love, may have power, together with all the saints, to grasp how wide and long and high and deep is the love of Christ, and to know this love that surpasses knowledge—that you may be filled to the measure of all the fullness of God.

God's unselfish love is the most precious of all the lessons I have ever learned. He does not accept us on the basis of what we can do for Him but because of what He can do for us. In fact, the very best and most successful of His servants are inadequate to the task.

Our Lord Jesus said to His disciples in Luke 17:10: "So likewise you, when you have done all those things which you are commanded, say, 'We are unprofitable servants. We have done what was our duty to do' " (NKJV).

We acquire infinitely more benefits from the Lord than He does from us. Our relationship with the Lord is based on love. The only good works acceptable to God are those that are motivated by our love for Him. Hebrews 6:10 says, "For God is not unjust to forget your work and labor of love which you have shown toward His name, in that you have ministered to the saints, and do minister" (NKJV).

All of our works will be tested by fire at the judgment seat of Christ. Our successful endeavors that were motivated by self-love and personal egotism are compared to wood, hay and stubble that can't survive the test of fire. All those efforts will burn up and we will suffer the loss. On the other hand, all our labors, even the unsuccessful ones, that were motivated by our love for the Lord Jesus are like gold, silver and precious gems. They will survive the testing fire. We will be rewarded for our labors of love, even for those ill-conceived efforts that failed to achieve anything worthwhile for God's kingdom.

Rejecting God's Love Leads to Tragedy

God has a specific plan for each of our lives, but He doesn't force it on us. We can insist on going our own way and follow our own plans to our ultimate regret.

> This is what the LORD says—
>   your Redeemer, the Holy One of Israel:

> "I am the LORD your God,
> who teaches you what is best for you,
> who directs you in the way you should go.
> If only you had paid attention to my commands,
> your peace would have been like a river,
> your righteousness like the waves of the sea."
> (Isaiah 48:17-18)

I remember well the husband of my first convert to Christ in one of my churches. His wife came down to the altar, weeping her way to God. Later I experienced the joy of leading her husband to Christ. They were growing well in Christ by leaps and bounds. One day her husband came to see me, obviously upset about something. He blurted out, "God told me to give up my pipe. There is no way that I am going to do it. My pipe is like an old friend. Who is God to tell me what to do?" I tried to reason with my friend by explaining that when he accepted Christ, God became his Father. I read Hebrews 12:9-11 to him:

> Moreover, we have all had human fathers who disciplined us and we respected them for it. How much more should we submit to the Father of our spirits and live! Our fathers disciplined us for a little while as they thought best; but God disciplines us for our good, that we may share in his holiness. No discipline seems pleasant at the time, but painful. Later on, however, it produces a harvest of righteousness and peace for those who have been trained by it.

I then counseled him to submit to the heavenly Father's discipline, but without success. He left my office in a huff. There was no softening in his attitude. The real issue was not his smoking habit, but his unwillingness to submit to the authority of his heavenly Father. His wife later explained how he had resented his earthly father's discipline. His attendance at church became erratic as his resentment grew.

A few months later, apparently without warning, he announced to his wife that he was going to leave her and the children because he did not love her anymore. "We married too young," he explained as his analysis of the situation. As he walked out of their lives, her tears and pleading did not stop him. Those were desperate, heartrending days for his wife and children.

After two years, her husband showed up at her doorstep. He admitted his foolishness and asked to be taken back. "Sorry. It's too late," she replied. "If only you had returned a few months ago, I would have welcomed you back. But now I have found a good man who really loves me."

Years later, while visiting my former church, I phoned my friend to see how he was doing. He told me, "Pastor, I have ruined my life. I have been unhappy for years." My heart went out to my friend. His life would have been so much better if he had only submitted himself to his heavenly Father's authority. God leads us step by step into His wonderful plan for our lives, but it is up to us to follow Him. The Bible reveals the way to success in life in Proverbs 16:3, "Commit to the LORD whatever you do, and your plans will succeed."

God Keeps His Promises

When I was fourteen years of age, I came to faith in Jesus by just hearing about Him, but now fifty-seven years later, I can say by experience that Jesus is true and faithful. No philosophical or theological argument could ever sway me away from Jesus, the true Messiah of Israel. At the time I accepted Jesus, I did not know that He had a specific plan for my life that if I would trust and follow Him I would have an amazing future.

I remember one special day fifty-seven years ago when, as a fourteen-year-old, I was sitting on the steps of the entrance of the Gospel Meeting House. I was waiting patiently for a black brother who came faithfully to open up the mission doors an hour before the services began. Brother Taylor liked to say, "I would rather be a doorkeeper in the house of my God than dwell in the tents of the wicked" (Psalm 84:10).

As I sat there, I was thinking about my uncertain future with a great deal of apprehension. I wished that I could peek into the future and see what kind of life I would live. In my wildest imagination, I did not expect such an amazing and fruitful life. My decision at the time was to leave my future in His hands.

As I am finishing my life's story of God's never-ending love, I have asked myself some serious questions.

What if I had decided not to accept Jesus as my Savior? I could have said, "I am a Jew and I have been taught that Jews aren't supposed to believe in Jesus."

What if I had resisted placing myself under the authority of Jesus? Suppose I had said, "I want to live my own life, in my own way. I don't want to be told what to do."

What if I had not trusted Jesus to heal my body? I know many people who refuse to pray for healing. Some conclude they are meant to suffer.

What if I had refused to get an education? I had many reasons to question the wisdom of going back to school. I had previously failed academically.

What if I had not married the godly woman of God's choice?

What if I had decided not to go into the ministry or if I had quit during difficulties? I could have made up all kinds of justifiable excuses, but if I had, I would never have discovered the faithfulness of Jesus in my life. All my decisions to trust the Lord with my life became milestones toward a meaningful and successful life. The best decision I ever made was to trust Jesus completely with my life.

God's Universal Invitation

Some difficult questions must be raised for consideration. What did my Jewish forefathers overlook in their search for God? What is the missing element in Judaism? I believe it is the truth of God's eternal sacrifice for sin predicted in Isaiah 53.

Few Jewish people are acquainted with this messianic prophecy because it is neglected and no longer read publicly in the synagogue. Every week at the Sabbath service a portion from the five books of Moses is read aloud along with a portion from the prophets. When the reader comes to Isaiah 52:12 and the entire chapter of Isaiah 53, he skips over it to chapter 54.

Why is it no longer read publicly? The reason for the omission of this Scripture goes back to the Jewish insurrection under Bar Kokhba, who led a bitter but unsuccessful revolt against Rome in 135 A.D. Up until then, messianic congregations were growing up throughout the Middle East. They were becoming a significant force in Israel. Jewish Christians called themselves Nazarenes because they believed in the messiahship and deity of Jesus of Nazareth. The Nazarenes freely joined in the weekly worship in the synagogue. Whenever Isaiah 53 was read, the Nazarenes spoke up and proclaimed Jesus.

Bar Kokhba asked the Nazarenes to join in his insurrection against the Emperor Hadrian. They refused because Bar Kokhba claimed to be the messiah. They called him "Bar Koziba," meaning "a liar." They predicted that Bar

Kokhba would lead Israel to a tragic defeat. Because of their refusal to join in the fight, Rabbi Akiva, who supported the messianic claims of Bar Kokhba, excommunicated the Nazarenes from the synagogue services. For the first time in the history of the synagogue, Isaiah 53 was excluded from the public reading of Scripture. Rabbi Akiva also added a nineteenth article to the ancient prayer called the Eighteen Benedictions. It was a condemnation on Jewish Christians.

A revival of Jewish believers in Jesus is happening again. All around the world, including Israel, Jews are turning to Jesus, their true Messiah. Whenever I have the opportunity to share my faith with an orthodox Jew or a rabbi, I would write out Isaiah 53:3-6 on a piece of paper and then ask the person to read it aloud.

> He was despised and rejected by men,
> a man of sorrows, and familiar with suffering.
> Like one from whom men hide their faces
> he was despised, and we esteemed him not.
>
> Surely he took up our infirmities
> and carried our sorrows,
> yet we considered him stricken by God,
> smitten by him, and afflicted.
> But he was pierced for our transgressions,
> he was crushed for our iniquities;
> the punishment that brought us peace
> was upon him,
> and by his wounds we are healed.
> We all, like sheep, have gone astray,
> each of us has turned to his own way;
> and the LORD has laid on him
> the iniquity of us all.

I would then ask the question, "Who is this speaking about?"

In over ninety percent of the cases, the reply would be, "It is speaking about Jesus."

I would then ask him, "Who do you think composed this statement about Jesus?"

"Did you?" he would ask me.

When I replied, "No!" my Jewish friend would guess again.

"Is it from the New Testament?"

By this time the situation becomes quite tense as I come to the answer. "No, it is from our own Jewish prophet, Isaiah. He prophesied of Jesus' suffering and death for our sins 700 years before Jesus was born into this world."

Rabbinic Judaism is not biblical Judaism because it contradicts the Torah. In A.D. 70, Rabbi Ben Zakkai escaped Jerusalem before the Romans destroyed it. He surrendered to Titus, the Roman general, and was granted permission to start an academy to train disciples. Many refer to him as the founder of Rabbinic Judaism. He was the first Jewish teacher ever to say that because the Temple was destroyed, blood sacrifices were no longer necessary for atonement of sins. Ben Zakkai asserted that a person can atone for his sins by just doing good deeds. He contradicted the very Torah he claimed to defend.

Moses wrote in Leviticus 17:11: "For the life of the flesh is in the blood: and I have given it to you upon the altar to make atonement for your souls: for it is the blood that maketh an atonement for the soul" (KJV).

Rabbinic Judaism has no valid sacrifice for sin. Why would God allow the Temple to be destroyed, which meant the end of blood atoning sacrifices for sin? It was because the eternal sacrifice of God's Son was accomplished on the altar of the cross on Mount Calvary. The sacrifices of bulls and goats were only as prophetic object lessons of the coming sacrifice of the true Lamb of God who takes away the sins of the world. Jesus is the only way to the heavenly Father because there is no other atonement for sin available. True Christianity is the fulfillment of biblical Judaism.

An invitation that comes from God through the prophet Isaiah must be taken seriously.

" 'Come now, let us reason together,' says the LORD. 'Though your sins are like scarlet, they shall be as white as snow; though they are red as crimson, they shall be like wool' " (Isaiah 1:18).

As I get older, being a Jew means more to me than ever before. I am thankful that I came to faith in the Jewish Messiah. Through Jesus I have found forgiveness of sins, peace with God and a wonderfully fulfilling life, which God offers to everyone who will put their trust in Him.

I frequently wondered why the Bible was not written as a systematic theology. Instead it is a collection of stories of people who experienced God in unique ways. In my early days of ministry, I tried to convince people to believe in Jesus through theological arguments. For the record, I had very poor results until I introduced them to the living Jesus. The evidence of His presence is too real to be denied. He satisfies the hungry heart and the seeking soul. My life story is about my experiences of fifty-seven years with God through Jesus. The invitation to experience Jesus is extended to everyone who wants it.

> [Jesus] was in the world, and though the world was made through him, the world did not recognize him. He came to that which was his own, but his own did not receive him. Yet to all who received

> him, to those who believed in his name, he gave the right to become children of God. (John 1:10-12)

My prayer is that the readers of my story will be persuaded to trust Jesus with their lives as well.

Albert Runge grew up in the tenements of Brooklyn, New York. In spite of poor health, "very little possibility of ever amounting to much" and "few academic skills," he studied at five institutions of higher learning including Houghton College and Fuller Seminary. His ministry included pastoring four churches in the U.S. and Canada, as well as extended preaching ministries at home and abroad. Albert and his wife, Lee, live in Abbotsford, British Columbia, Canada. They have four children and eleven grandchildren.